D0923997

THE ENTREPRENEURIAL LINGUIST

୨ଈ

THE BUSINESS-SCHOOL APPROACH TO FREELANCE TRANSLATION

୨ଈ

JUDY A. JENNER
AND
DAGMAR V. JENNER

୨ଈ

ILLUSTRATIONS BY
ALEJANDRO MORENO-RAMOS

The Entrepreneurial Linguist: The Business-School Approach to Freelance Translation
By Judy A. Jenner and Dagmar V. Jenner

ISBN 978-0-557-25623-5
First edition

© 2010 by Judy A. Jenner and Dagmar V. Jenner. All rights reserved.

Published by EL Press, a division of Twin Translations, LLC. It is illegal to reproduce or share any part of this book without explicit permission by the authors, Judy A. Jenner and Dagmar V. Jenner. This includes uploading and distribution via the internet or any other means. Short passages can be used for reviewing purposes. For any questions, please contact the authors at book@entrepreneuriallinguist.com. Your support of the authors' right is appreciated.

Disclaimer:
The authors have thoroughly researched all items discussed and have written this book in good faith and to the best of their abilities. However, readers should be advised that this work is also partially based on the authors' personal professional experience, which might or might not be representative. The authors are both professional linguists, but make no guarantee that any or all of the information in this book is either correct or applicable to all readers. We encourage fellow linguists to seek professional advice for any specific area, such as tax planning, accounting, or business structuring.

The use of the names of certain actual, well-known places, institutions and companies does not imply that those entities have any particular attributes or follow any particular practices, procedures or policies, depicted or otherwise. They are illustrative samples of business practices and have been used in good faith.

About the font:
This book as been laid out in Adobe InDesign CS4. The font is Minion Pro, an Adobe originals typeface created by Robert Slimbach. This font is based on the classical typefaces that are typical of the late Renaissance.

About the cover:
The cover is an original design by Ulf Buchholz.

We dedicate this book to all our talented, hard-working fellow linguists around the world.

TABLE OF CONTENTS

Think of yourself as a business • Advantages of working with a small business • Think of yourself as a customer •
Case study: the urgent project • Case study: deposits for large projects

Bank accounts • Should I hire a CPA? • Record keeping • Get organized
• Learn to love paperwork • Should I hire a bookkeeper? • Translation
Office 3000 • No procrastinating • Prompt invoicing • Mileage report
• Log every single mile • Sample logsheet • Decreasing your expenses
• Needs versus wants • Where to save • Office supplies • Ink • Paper •
Buy in bulk • Gadgets • Business phone and cellular phone • Alternative
phone options • Instant messaging • Postage • Coupons are your friend
• The library is your friend • What not to save on

Blogging • Benefits of having a blog • Should you have a blog? • Blogging platforms • Blog hosting options • RSS feeds • About Me • Blogging food for thought • How much time should I spend on it? • What
kinds of blog postings should I put up? • What kinds of blog postings
should I refrain from putting up? • Dealing with comments • Com-

menting on other blogs • Linking to other blogs • English-language translation blogs that we like • Should I put ads on my blog? • Micro-blogging services • Say it in 140 characters or less • Following others • Professional networks • Top picks for professional networks • Professional networks 101 • Additional LinkedIn applications, status updates, and daily digest • Social networks • Top pick for social network • Getting started on Facebook • Being smart and safe on Facebook

© 2009 Jenner – By Alejandro Moreno-Ramos

INTRODUCTION

There are many terms used to describe professionals who work in the languages industry. We are known as translators, interpreters, writers, academics, linguists, language service providers, etc. For this book, we have chosen the term "linguist," which comes from the Latin, where lingua means tongue or speech. Linguists are defined as individuals who have either studied linguistics or who are proficient in several languages. While most translators and interpreters might not have studied linguistics, but rather translation or languages, the second definition of the term linguist fits us very well. In this book, we will use the term "linguist" to mean "language services providers" or "translators and interpreters."

As linguists, we traditionally excel in the humanities. We have been trained to think as humanists and to pay close attention to language, nuances, syntax, and the art of translation. However, most linguists work as freelancers, which means, in essence, that they are running small businesses. Businesspersons, on the other hand, focus on plans, long-term results, growth, and revenue. They run their businesses efficiently while keeping their eye on the bottom line. Many freelance translators and interpreters, both those with degrees from translation institutes and those without, feel that they are ill-prepared for running a business upon graduation. For instance, one of our colleagues, a graduate of a prestigious translation program, was puzzled that her university offered no business advice on how to start a career as a freelance linguist. Upon graduation, the advice her university's career center gave her was to "try the Yellow Pages" to find clients. No business classes were offered during our friend's particular graduate program, nor are they offered in most translation and interpretation programs. Linguists are in good company with lawyers and doctors, who also obtain a wealth of profession-specific knowledge during their studies, but receive little or no training on how to run their businesses.

The big question is: how are we, as linguists, supposed to acquire the business skills that are necessary in order to run our practices efficiently, strategically, and successfully? Unfortunately, the answer had traditionally been: learning by doing. When we decided to start our business, Twin Translations, in 2002, there was little information to be found on the realities of running a translation and interpretation business. We discovered Corinne McKay's "How to Succeed as a Freelance Translator" (published in 2005) years later. It has since sold more than 3,500 copies and received outstanding reviews around the world. We want to build on Corinne's excellent work and go even more in-depth into the realities of running your own translation or interpretation business while being both an entrepreneur and a linguist: an entrepreneurial linguist.

Judy received her formal business training at the University of Nevada, Las Vegas (M.B.A., marketing, December 2001), while Dagmar has an academic background in languages (equivalent of M.A., University of Salzburg, Austria, French, 2000) and is enrolled in the master's program for conference interpreting (Spanish and Franch) at the University of Vienna, Austria. Dagmar is also currently writing her dissertation in Romance languages at the University of Vienna, focusing on the feminist discourse in the work of Chilean author Isabel Allende. We created this book by combining our formal academic knowledge with the practical skill set we have acquired through the aforementioned learning-by-doing method.

This book is a natural progression that started when we began writing our translation blog, Translation Times (www.translationtimes.com). In it, we mainly address the business side of translation. We have received many e-mails and comments from readers who have enjoyed the blog, thus prompting us to consider writing a book. After being encouraged by fellow linguists and after drafting many a marketing plan for colleagues, Judy turned the information she was sharing informally into a presentation called "Lessons from Business School: The Entrepreneurial Linguist," which she has presented successfully in both Europe and the U.S. Inspired by the positive feedback received in these workshops from Seattle to Vienna, we decided to base our book on the lessons presented in the "Entrepreneurial Linguist" workshop and stuck with the title. The idea and desire to write a work of non-fiction was a gradual process, and we began work on it in mid-2009. Readers of the American Translators Association's newsletter, the Chronicle, will also recognize some of the writing in this book, as Judy pens the monthly "Entrepreneurial Linguist" column for the Chronicle. Her writing, which mainly focuses on marketing and entrepreneurship, also frequently appears in the Institute of Translation and Interpreting's Bulletin.

This book is meant for both linguists who are already running their translation businesses and those who are just trying to get established. We presuppose that readers have the necessary skills and training to succeed as linguists. The intent is to give you the business skills you need – the ones you never learned – to succeed in this competitive market.

ACKNOWLEDGEMENTS

First and foremost, we would like to thank our parents, Dr. Alfred and Dr. Roswitha Jenner, and in particular our ex-pat father. We would not be in the profession we are today if it were not for our multicultural upbringing, courtesy of our parents. We will continue to cherish the tremendous gift of languages and culture that they have given us by allowing us to grow up in a multilingual household in Mexico City.

Without a doubt, Thomas Gruber is the main driving force behind our business. He has a bottomless knowledge of IT, search engine optimization, fantastic business ideas, endless patience and the ability to solve any computer-related problems. Thomas, who is also Dagmar's boyfriend, is the most creative thinker we know, and he is the guardian angel, IT superhero and marketing strategist behind Twin Translations. Judy's attorney husband, Keith Anderson, has been a tireless supporter of our business venture and has gone above and beyond to support us and the creation of this book, both financially and emotionally. We are truly appreciative of his quick wit and his spot-on insight into legal and fiscal matters.

When it came time to find an editor and layout professional for this book, we knew exactly whom to ask: our friend and longtime collaborator, journalist and photographer Ulf Buchholz. There are few friends in our lives who are as giving as Ulf. We are immensely grateful for his unconditional support, generosity, knowledge of the publishing world, journalism expertise, and friendship. In addition, our dear friend Greg Thilmont, an extraordinary writer, editor, and internet entrepreneur, volunteered to do the final edit. His special editing touch gave us the reassurance that this book was ready for publication.

Choosing the design for the cover was quite a challenge. Several friends, family members, and colleagues contributed some excellent ideas. We ultimately chose an elegant and simple design that Ulf Buchholz created for us. Our colleague, Spanish translator and cartoonist Alejandro Moreno-Ramos, who draws outstanding translation-centered cartoons, contributed all the illustrations in this book. He holds the copyright to all of them, minus the first cartoon, which he created specifically for this book. They feature Mox, the overeducated and underpaid translator, his sidekick, a turtle named Mina, Calvo, a senior translator, Pam, the evil project manager, and a parade of other characters. We are very grateful to Alejandro, who lives and works in Spain, for giving us the permission to reprint many of his cartoons. We are delighted with our Entrepreneurial Linguist cartoon, for which Alejandro would not accept payment. We would like to thank Alejandro for his generosity, endless creativity and ability to find humor in the everyday struggles linguists face. To see the entire collection of Alejandro's cartoons, please visit his frequently updated blog: http://mox.ingenierotraductor. com/.

We are also grateful to our extended family, friends, and colleagues around the world who have suggested we write (and continue writing and editing) this book, which took the better part of 2009 and early 2010.

HOW TO USE THIS BOOK

While business school does not prepare you to run a small business per se, it does give you formal structure and the ability to understand how the economy works. There is no specific roadmap taught, but by learning about the main subjects that influence the economy and the way businesses work in it – finance, economics, marketing, accounting, statistics, international business, etc. – you learn how to position and structure your business. Throughout the years, we have learned to apply these lessons to our translation practice. Our goal is to give our readers and colleagues the tools to do the same.

Fundamentally, business school is composed of two parts: academic theories and the case-study method. The most commonly used case studies are those published by the *Harvard Business Review*, and through them, students are encouraged to learn how companies failed or succeeded and to write reports on what they would have done differently. The cases are usually complex and include analyzing the company's financial situation in great detail. For our purposes as freelance linguists, we will reduce that information to what we can apply to our everyday businesses. We will discuss theory only briefly and then present a select number of case studies and many real-life examples from our own practices, colleagues' businesses, and other businesses outside our industries. We believe that our fellow linguists, who run small translation and interpretation businesses just like we do, need, above anything, practical advice that they can start using right away.

While this book frequently references the American market, the lessons contained here are mostly universal. In rare cases we refer to U.S.-specific issues, such as taxation, but they are few and far in between.

This book's main focus is on marketing, social media and web 2.0, pricing, entrepreneurship, accounting, professional development and work-life balance. The chapters are independent of each other, although the book as a whole is meant to work together. While we recommend that you read the book in its entirety, you can also simply read the chapters that interest you the most and then come back to other sections at your leisure. We have included many sub-headings and a detailed table of contents to make this book as user-friendly as possible. As entrepreneurs, the most important resource we truly have is our time, so it is our goal to help you use it in the most efficient way possible. When reading this book, it will be apparent that there is significant overlap between areas, and that is the way we inteded it. We frequently refer back to other chapters, and the astute reader will soon realize that many of the elements of entrepreneurship are interdependent.

This book is written for those linguists who want to work with direct clients, which is the sole focus of our translation work. We did not include advice and tips on how to work with translation agencies, but a wealth of information is available on that topic from other sources.

This book was written for linguists of all skill levels and focuses on the practical side of running a translation business in any language combination. It is intended to be easily accessible reading material for linguists who want to be entrepreneurs. While running a business is a serious matter, the tone of this book is purposefully informal and non-academic.

How To Use This Book

http://mox.ingenierotraductor.com

© 2009 Alejandro Moreno-Ramos

CHAPTER 1

§•

THE NEW MINDSET

Think of yourself as a business

The first thing you need to do is to stop thinking of yourself as "just" a freelance linguist and to start thinking of yourself as a business. You are selling your services; therefore, you are a business. Start behaving like one! A one-person business run out of a spare room is just as legitimate a business as a Fortune 500 company. Most of your transactions will most likely be on the business-to-business (B2B) level, and you are an equal partner in those transactions. Even if you are the only person working for your small business, give yourself a pat on the back; welcome to being an entrepreneur! If you live in the U.S. and need help with getting a business license, finding out where to file specific fees, or have other questions about starting your business, consider using the free services of the Small Business Administration (SBA, www.sba.gov). In addition, take advantage of the services offered by SCORE (www.score.org), including detailed advice from retired executives who can help you with anything from creating a business plan to requesting a loan. SCORE works closely with the SBA. While the vast majority of the services offered by the SBA and SCORE are free of charge, they do offer several fee-based workshops on important topics such as accounting, marketing, etc. The fees are usually quite reasonable.

Have you ever been intimidated when negotiating with a potential client because you were "just" a freelance translator, as if that were not a tremendous accomplishment? It is challenging not to be intimidated when negotiating with a company such as IBM or Target. However, the legitimacy and seriousness of a business does not depend on its size. Just because a corporation is large does not make it more respectable, more reputable, nor does it make it immune to failure, as we have seen in the last few years. On the flip side, just because a business is small does not mean that it should not be taken seriously or that it is not respectable or reputable. Quite the contrary: the U.S. business world is made up largely of small businesses. Small businesses represent 99.7% of the U.S. economy.[1] In addition, one-person businesses account for a staggering 78% of all U.S. businesses.[2] So regardless of whether you are a solo translator, you work in a translator group with a few business partners, or you work in a translation team with your best friend: start thinking of yourself as a business. From the customer's point of view, there are quite a lot of advantages to working with a small business.

Advantages of working with a small business

&. **Direct contact with the decision makers**. Customers are able to speak directly to the owner(s) and do not have to jump through hoops and multiple layers of assistants, phone transfers, dozens of e-mails from subordinates, and voicemail messages.

&. **Immediate decision-making**. Have you ever dealt with a large company for anything, be it a service call on your air conditioning unit, a call to your credit card company, or trying to get in touch with a real person in the billing department of an insurance company? It is tedious and time-consuming, and someone usually has to check with someone else on nearly everything. Small businesses are much more nimble, efficient, and can make decisions very quickly, because most of the time the owner is the chief decision maker, CFO, head of human resources, chief technology expert, chief data filer, etc. Large companies appreciate dealing with small businesses that are highly professional, reliable, flexible, and respond quickly to changing market demands and customer requests.

&. **Cost savings**. Even if your rates are high, you can be fairly certain that your rates as a small business are much more affordable than a larger company's. The main reason is that larger companies have to account for their significant overhead costs, such as rent, utilities, salaries, etc. Although these costs are, of course, not billed directly to the potential client, a large company needs to take all these costs into account when it quotes on a project, especially salaries. The only payroll most of us need to meet is our own.

Now that you know some of the things your clients might appreciate about a small business, start developing some pride in what you do and the services you offer. There is no reason to be intimidated when working with large clients. Think

---

1 http://www.sba.gov/advo/stats/sbfaq.pdf
2 http://smallbiztrends.com/2007/07/single-person-businesses-booming.html

about it this way: you provide a professional, highly specialized service that is in demand with customers all over the globe. Why should you be intimidated by the industry giants? After all, your potential client, industry giant or not, contacted you because they are interested in your services. A caveat: in an effort to make their company or business look much larger than it is, sometimes linguists draft marketing texts and websites with the pronoun "we" in it – as in "we offer top-notch translation and interpretation services." Resist the temptation to do so. Do not talk about the company owners in plural if there is only one and do not list contact e-mails as sales@spanishtranslator.com and invoicing@spanishtranslator.com if these are all going to the same address. Do not be ashamed of being only one person. As a matter of fact, pretending to have several people at your business rather than just the one is misleading and unethical. Be upfront with the fact that you are a very small business.

Think of yourself as a customer

The second thing you need to do is to think of yourself as a customer. Now that you have started thinking of yourself as a business, put yourself in the customer's shoes. If you were a customer, what would you want? This is a question that you should be asking yourself frequently. Your goal is to make things easy for your customers and to build solid working relationships. If you do not know what a customer wants, ask. We have this line on sticky notes on our desks, and every time someone calls or e-mails for a price quote, we ask ourselves: "If we were the person on the other side of the transaction, what would we want?" Seeing any business from your customer's point of view is a powerful tool.

It is sometimes difficult to find the right balance between what we want and what our customers want. Let us start with what we, as business owners, most likely want. Here is a short, by no means all inclusive, list:

ᘓ **We want to make a living.** We do not run charities. Rather, we run small businesses that need to make a profit.

ᘓ **We want to feel valued as professional service providers.** This includes being treated with the respect that any vendor deserves.

ᘓ **We like to set our own schedules.** Some of us are morning people who subscribe to the "early bird catches the worm" philosophy, while others are complete night owls and enjoy working from midnight to 8 a.m. while guzzling energy drinks.

We like to be able to decide who we work with. One of the great pleasures of running your own business is that you do not have to accept every project that comes across your desk. If you worked in a traditional, non-entrepreneurial setting before, you surely remember having to do work for superiors, or even colleagues, whose ideas might not have been good or feasible, yet you had to implement them. Now you can decide if you would like to accept or decline a project. Neither decision will not cost you a promotion.

We like to take vacations on our terms. Do you want to take the weekend off to go hiking in Yellowstone? What if you decide to stay an extra day? There are no vacation slips to fill out and no bosses to notify. Just turn in that urgent translation before you hit the road, notify all your clients, and if needed, take your laptop with you.

We like being our own bosses. The freedom to make your own decisions and to not have to rely on someone else's decision-making is very important to most freelance linguists.

We sometimes like working in our pajamas. If you could have done it when you worked in a traditional office setting, you would have done it, too, correct? Now that you can, why not work in your bathing suit in your backyard if you have wireless internet? Work does not have to be restricted to a specific time, place, or dress code. Feel free to reinvent the wheel: there are no limits to where you can work. Dress however you like. The main exception to this is when you meet with customers. You should always dress professionally for face-to-face interactions.

However, running your own business comes with a tremendous amount of responsibility. First and foremost, you must remember that your success will depend on your ability to attract clients and to make them happy. Without clients, you do not have a business. Then you would have to change out of your pajamas, put on a power suit, print out some résumés and look for a job as an in-house translator or interpreter. You would most likely work in a traditional office environment, with a boss, a hierarchy, office rules, gossip, and fridges full of moldy lunch containers with labels on them. If you do not want that, then keep your customers happy.

Now let us think about what customers want. You should analyze each situation separately and never stop asking: "What would my customer want?" Here are a few things that customers are likely to want. Those things will be the minimum requirements that you need to meet in order to keep your customers happy.

🕭 **Customers want professional services from a professional company.** This includes answering the phone professionally and having a well-designed website. You should create an environment in which the customer can feel comfortable and well taken care of.

🕭 **Customers want clear and precise answers.** Do not beat around the bush. Answer questions truthfully and clearly. Give customers the information they need in order to make informed purchasing decisions.

🕭 **Customers want their deadlines met.** Delivering quality work on time is the minimum requirement in any profession, especially if you would like referrals.

🕭 **Customers do not necessarily want to be educated, unless it is very gently.** Think of yourself as a customer. When you call your mechanic because there is smoke coming out of your car's engine, you do not want to be lectured about the finer points of engine-building, especially in terms you do not understand. You want to know what the problem is, whether you could have prevented it, and how much it will cost to fix it. Buyers of translation and interpretation services want the same thing. They might not know what a source language is, nor do they need to know that. It is our job to clearly define the industry-specific terms that the client might not be familiar with, to explain how the process works, and to enable the customer to make good decisions. Make things simple and easy to understand for your customer.

🕭 **Customers want to know the exact terms of the services they are buying.** Include as much information as possible in your written price quotes, such as delivery time, precise cost breakdown, documents needed from the customer to finish the project, terms and conditions, etc. All this should be put in writing for the benefit of both parties. Be sure to have customers sign the quote before you commence work.

🕭 **Customers want to know your qualifications.** Do not wait for the customer to ask about your qualifications. Rather, disclose them early on. Tell your potential customers exactly how you are an expert in the field. List previous experience, topic-specific knowledge, and mention previous clients. Please see the marketing chapter for details on this.

🕭 **Customers want you to be available to answer questions.** As a small-business owner, your customers should be your first priority. Be available and return calls and e-mails promptly.

Customers want open lines of communication. You might very well be the last step in a long list of individuals who have cooperated on a project, so keep the customer informed of your progress, even if it is just a quick e-mail or phone call. If you have questions, ask. A vendor who never asks any questions could be perceived as not being detail-oriented enough. It is impossible to know every company-specific acronym. Do not spend hours searching for something your customer could answer in sixty seconds off the top of her head. Communication is the key to successful collaborations.

Now that we have looked at what you want and what your customers want, we should look at what happens when there is a conflict between the two. You have to make concessions and compromises in order to run a business. Just because you are your own boss does not mean you can play exclusively by your own rules, especially if they conflict with a customer's.

Case study: the urgent project

It is 5 p.m. on a Wednesday evening and a client calls with an urgent project that is due the following day. You have no plans for the evening, but you would rather just relax. However, it is your favorite client and they appear to be in a serious bind. You are in the position to be able to help them solve their problem. Should you stay up all night to accommodate your client?

Think of yourself as a business (making yourself and your bank account happy): You had been looking forward to a quiet evening at home. Part of the benefit of being self-employed is that you do not have to accept every job that comes your way. You value your free time, but you also value your customer and their business.

Think of yourself as a customer (making your client happy): Your customer would certainly understand if you are not available. On the other hand, it would make for a very appreciative client if you were able to accept this job. Helping a good customer out when they need you and proving to be a vendor who will go the extra mile for them will strengthen your relationship.

Potential compromise solution (making both you and the customer happy): Unless you are extremely tired and do not think you could give this project the time, attention, and focus it deserves, you should go ahead and accept the project. However, you should apply the additional charge for the 24-hour turnaround. This is quite common for many professional services, and few professionals will expect you to work through the night for the same price that you would during the day.

Case study: deposits for large projects

It is Monday morning and a new customer, who works for a large company, contacts you with a 50,000 word translation request. Your week looks fairly open. You are not familiar with this customer, but she comes highly recommended by one of your repeat customers, who assures you that this customer is trustworthy and has an excellent payment history. It is your policy to request partial payment up front from new customers, especially for a large translation that would require committing several weeks of your time exclusively to the project. Your potential customer reacts negatively to the required initial deposit, but is willing to pay 30% at the half-point of the translation.

⟨ **Think of yourself as a business** (making yourself and your bank account happy): This customer is a direct client, so it is nearly impossible to obtain a record on her payment history with vendors. Your regular policy is to ask for 30% up front prior to commencing work for a large project of this magnitude, with 30% due at the half-point of the translation and 40% due upon delivery. You have yet to make an exception to this rule, and you have always received payment.

⟨ **Think of yourself as a customer** (making your client happy): Many customers do not like to pay ahead of time for a service, especially if they work for a large company. Traditionally, accounting departments pay invoices after services have been rendered, and your contact person might not want to approach the accounting department with a special request.

⟨ **Potential compromise solution** (making both you and the customer happy): You inform your potential customer of your pricing policy and explain to her that you are a small business, but that thanks to your current customer's recommendation, you will make an exception and waive the initial deposit. Do not forget to require the customer's signature on your price quote, where you clearly state your payment terms. By signing the quote, the customer will have agreed to your payment terms.

CHAPTER 2

&

ORGANIZATION & ACCOUNTING

Accounting was a challenging subject in business school, because it included working through complex financial data for real-life companies, which meant having to create highly sophisticated spreadsheets connected to each other via dozens and dozens of files. It was good preparation for the infinitely simpler task of keeping track of income and expenses for our very small business. A note on taxes: we are not qualified to give you tax advice nor do we intend to do so in this chapter. Please contact your local tax professional for in-depth advice. Organization goes hand-in-hand with good accounting practices. Being highly organized in your accounting and other business-related tasks will make your more efficient.

Bank accounts

First things first: you must have a separate checking and/or savings account for your business. These accounts can either be in your personal name, or ideally in your company's name. In the U.S., in order to get an account in your business name, you must show a business license and a federal EIN number, which is issued by the Internal Revenue Service. The most important thing is that you keep your personal and your business funds separate. Of course, you will be paying yourself from your business account – and how you do that depends on the type of company you have – but you should not co-mingle funds. You should also apply for a separate business credit card so you can make all your business-related purchases on it. Many banks around the world offer favorable terms for small businesses, so check with your favorite bank. Ideally, get a credit card that lets you earn points that you can either redeem for cash or items that might be beneficial for your business. It is quite possible that you might pull out the wrong credit card, say, your personal card when you are really making a business purchase. If you do that, you should reimburse your personal account quickly before you forget about the transaction. Keeping your accounts separate will greatly facilitate your accounting and will make your life easier once tax time rolls around. If you are looking for very good banking terms in the U.S., try a local credit union. Most banks do offer free or low-cost checking accounts for small businesses.

Should I hire a CPA?

This is a question that comes up frequently in translation circles. Traditionally, we have hired two CPAs – one in Vienna for the European side of our business, and one in the U.S. for the American side. For simplicity's sake, we will only address tax preparation here and will not go into the other issues CPAs can help you with, including accounting and long-term planning. We had decided several years ago that we were much better off outsourcing the taxes to someone who is a pro and use the time we "gained" to work on what we excel at – translation. However, for the American side of our business, that recently changed. While interviewing potential CPAs, we were quite underwhelmed by their expertise, and did not really feel that they would add substantial value to the process. In this case, by value we mean that the CPA would be able to find us significant tax deductions that we did not know about, hence saving us money. None of the CPAs we spoke to had a clear rate sheet, and we were not given specific price quotes for the services we were requesting. The main issue for us was not price. If the service were good and added value, we would be happy to pay the going rate. However, since we had the strong (but perhaps incorrect) feeling that the CPA would simply plug the numbers into a tax preparation software, we decided to buy the tax software (TurboTax, in our case, http://turbotax.intuit.com/) ourselves. We have been quite happy with the results. For the European side, we have retained our CPA, as she does an exceptional job and she makes the process very simple for us. As long as you can find a CPA who meets your needs, it is always advisable to trust your finances and taxes to a professional rather than doing it all yourself.

A good cost calculation would be to estimate the number of hours that it would take you to do your taxes based on how long it has taken you in the past, multiply that by what you can make per hour, on average, and compare that figure to what a professional tax preparer would charge you.

Tax preparation fees vary depending on whether you are a sole proprietor, an LLC, an S-Corp, etc., but you need to expect to pay at least several hundred dollars a year.

While the odds of getting audited in the U.S. are low, having a professional prepare your taxes will give you peace of mind and offer you better protection in case of an audit. In addition, professional tax preparers keep abreast of all changes in taxation, which could save you significant amounts of money.

If you are not quite ready to do your own taxes but do not want the expense of a CPA, try a tax preparation service, which are quite common in the U.S.

Record keeping

To maintain good accounting practices, you must keep good records. This means saving all your receipts and insisting on getting receipts for every business-related expense, no matter how small, even if that means that the Starbucks attendant, who automatically throws the receipt in the trash, has to dig it out. The best way to do this is to have a separate compartment in your wallet where you collect all the business-related receipts. Log them in a simple spreadsheet on a daily or weekly basis. If you are a woman and carry a purse, you could also consider having a separate small envelope for your receipts. According to one of our favorite tax books, "Lower Your Taxes – Big Time!" by Sandy Botkin, the IRS does not require receipts for purchases under $75, but it is a good idea to collect all receipts and keep them in a safe place just in case.

Get organized

This is probably one of the most crucial things you can do for yourself. There are many great ways to organize your paperwork, and fellow translators have shared their ideas about this for years. We are talking about paperwork that you have in the form of physical papers, including:

- Receipts for purchases you have made while meeting with clients.

- Company-related bills , such as cell phone bills or web hosting expenses.

- Deposit slips from ATM machines documenting deposits (mark the client's name and project on the receipt to allow for easy filing).

- Receipts from government-related expenses, such as filing fees for your business permit.

- Invoices that have been issued to you by subcontractors, if any.

- Cancelled checks if you receive them.

We store all our receipts in inexpensive, colorful boxes that we can easily label. Inside these boxes, we keep four envelopes – one for each quarter of the year. After we log a receipt in our income statement spreadsheet, we put a checkmark on the receipt, initial it, and put the date that we recorded it on it. Should we ever be audited, we can just pull out all the receipts by quarter, accompanied by the corresponding spreadsheet. The physical receipts will serve as back-up should you be audited, but your or your CPA will need your electronic spreadsheet (or other software program) with logging of the expenses and income when it is time to do your taxes. Make back-up files of your electronic data, because you will need that information during tax season. There are several good options for backing up your data, including online back-up services and external hard drives.

Learn to love paperwork

While doing paperwork is traditionally not that much fun, there is something to be said for a little bit of painless, mindless, repetitive work once in a while to relax your brain from linguistic challenges. It can be a nice little break to take 10 minutes every day and log our receipts and expenses. We actually enjoy it because it because we can see instant results, we get things off our desks, and we feel instantly more organized and on top of our finances. Embrace your inner organizational goddess and make peace with paperwork. It is important to have all the paperwork nice and organized, not only to give you control over your finances, but also in case you ever get audited. In addition, we work much better when our desks are nice and clean and it feels like we can think freely.

Also, think of yourself as the entrepreneur you are. Do you know what your accounts receivable are? Do you know what your accounts payable are? You do not have to know this data off the top of your head, but you should know where to find that information very quickly. Unless you are running a large, highly profitable operation, you will most likely be doing the paperwork yourself. Being self-employed means that you get to do whatever you would like with your business's funds, but it also means that you should be on top of them at all times. If you were an in-house translator or interpreter before you ran your own business, you probably remember thinking once in a while: "Well, it is not my money. I think the company is making a poor decision, but it is not my money." Now it is your money. Spend it wisely, know how much you have, and manage it well.

Should I hire a bookkeeper?

If you are somewhat savvy with numbers and organized enough, you can certainly forego hiring a bookkeeper and do it yourself. The main thing a bookkeeper would do is log and organize the receipts that you bring her and keep running totals of your expenses, which you can do yourself easily enough in about an hour a week, depending on how many individual transactions have to be logged. Consider purchasing easy-to-use accounting software, either fee-based or open source (typically free). Some people prefer outsourcing these tasks and show up at their bookkeeper's office once a month with a shoebox full of receipts. Personally, we enjoy tracking our expenses and income daily, and it is relatively little work that would not justify the expense for us. However, if you really dislike doing paperwork and your time could be used more efficiently by doing something else, then you should outsource this task. It is all about opportunity cost: the time that you use logging your receipts could perhaps be used for other, potentially more lucrative things. It is a decision you should make early on before things become too overwhelming. Do not wait until your receipts spill onto the floor before deciding how to handle your bookkeeping. Beyond organizing your receipts, bookkeepers and/or accountants can also assist you with much more complex tasks such as payroll.

Translation Office 3000

Translation Office 3000 (also known as TO) is a powerful translator-specific software program designed to manage your invoices, clients, and projects. It will not replace your electronic record-keeping for expenses, and it retails for roughly $250 (http://www.translation3000.com/). TO can quickly and accurately create professional price quotes. The word-counting software Anycount is integrated into the program. In addition, TO keeps track of all your current projects, issues template-based invoices, and gives you a precise overview of accounts receivable at any time. There is some work required in defining all the settings. The interface needs some improvement, and some advanced functions, such as the ability to create customized invoice templates, require some higher-level tech skills. The program is database-driven, and it is also an excellent tool to keep all your customers' information in one place, including phone numbers, addresses, e-mail addresses as well as additional information such as customized prices for specific clients.

No procrastinating

Some of the best advice we ever received from our CPA is to not let the receipts and information you need to log in your spreadsheets pile up, especially if you are returning from a business trip and have many receipts. The more things you have piled up on your desk, the less likely you will be to actually tackle the paperwork. It might be tough, but do it anyway. Reward yourself with an ice cream bar, a run with the dog, an hour of reading on the porch, or anything else that you look forward to. Bribe yourself if you must, but get those receipts off your desk. In addition to making your life easier, it is also advantageous to do this right away because you might not remember all the details later, including the name of the person you went to lunch with, what the business purpose was and how much you tipped the valet parking attendant, etc. This is information that you will need to provide the IRS in case of an audit.

Prompt invoicing

We do not know about you, but writing invoices and billing customers is one of our favorite activities. It gives a project closure and sets us up to receive payment for our services. However, many linguists do not invoice their clients in a timely manner, either because they are too busy or because they forget about it. Other linguists want to give their clients more time to pay the invoices, so they issue the invoices a significant time after the services have been rendered. However, that is generally not a good idea, as you might negatively impact the company's accounting practices. For instance, in a previous job, Judy occasionally outsourced services, including translation services, to vendors. Some of these individuals would take months to invoice, which had the unfortunate result of getting Judy in trouble with the accounting department. You are not doing your customers any favors by not billing them promptly, and they certainly do not want to receive invoices months later. One vendor billed several months later: in a new calendar year. Needless to say, accounting strongly advised Judy not to work with that vendor again. Remember that your goal should be to receive prompt payment for your services and to have steady cash flow, and that includes invoicing your customer in a timely manner.

Mileage report

If you are running a full-time freelance business and your main place of business is your primary residence, then you can log every mile driven for that business from your house. If you are not logging every single mile that you drive for business, you are selling yourself short and making less money because you will be claiming fewer tax deductions. Here is a partial, non-exhaustive list of trips that you should be tracking as business expenses:

- Driving to the post office to mail files and presents to clients and business partners.

- Trips to meetings with contractors, such as lawyers and CPAs.

- Driving to the bank to deposit business checks.

- Going to see clients for meetings, lunches, dinners, and other client events.

- Trips to the copy shop and office supply store.

- Trips to the airport for business trips.

In the U.S., the current mileage reimbursement rate for 2010, as set by the Internal Revenue Service, is 50 cents per business mile driven. For more details on this, please visit their website: http://www.irs.gov/. The IRS increases or decreases the mileage rate yearly, depending on a variety of factors (fuel costs, etc.) For instance, the rate decreased between 2008 and 2009, because the cost of fuel was higher in 2008 than it was in 2009. At the end of the calendar year, check the IRS's rate for the following year.

Log every single mile

This might sound tedious, but once you have set up your system, the process will be simple and quick. Even if you just drive four miles somewhere, that is $2. We do not know about you, but we will gladly take it. Remember that you are running a small business, and that many countries, including the U.S., have favorable tax laws for those who take the risk of running their own businesses. For the details of mileage tax deduction in other countries, please ask your tax professional or consult the respective country's tax code to ensure you are doing everything right. There is no such thing as "I did not know about it" when you are self-employed. It is your job to know.

Sample logsheet

There are several different ways to log business mileage that are accepted by the IRS. We have found that it is easiest to log every single trip, including the beginning and ending odometer reading of your car. There are many folks online who will want to sell you their "IRS fool-proof" Excel spreadsheet for $20, which sounds quite overpriced to us. We quickly created our own spreadsheet, and are happy to share it with you here. It includes a sample of a typical mileage entry.

Starting: 1-Jan-10		Ending: 31-Dec-10				
Date	Beginning Odometer	Ending Odometer	Destination	Miles	Additional details	
6-Jan-10	64975	64990	Groovy Beans 2579 Cactus Bloom Lane, LV, NV 89489: meeting with client Adele Mission González, VP of Marketing, FRZM International	15	None	
			Total monthly miles	15		
			IRS mileage rate ($0.50/mile for 2010)	$0.50		
			Total monthly mileage deduction	$7.50		

Decreasing your expenses

One strategy for making more take-home money is, of course, to bill more and to sell more of your services. Since profit is the difference between your income and expenses, there is also another way to make more profit without increasing your income: decreasing your expenses. This is something that, as freelancers, we do not think about that much, as most of us have fairly modest expenses. However, even small changes can make a big difference in the long term.

Needs versus wants

Speaking of expenses: there are things you really need and things that you merely want for your business. Some things are nice to have, but are not essential for running a business. The decision about what you want and what you need is entirely up to you, but remember that you are running a small business. Even if you can take a tax deduction for certain purchases, that does not mean that the product or service is free.

Here is the bare minimum of what you will need in order to run a successful translation or interpretation business:

- A computer

- A printer, ideally with integrated scanner and regular supplies for it

- A well-designed, ergonomic chair

- A phone (landline or cellular or both)

- A word processing and spreadsheet software package

- If you use them, translation memory tools (TM), also known as computer-assisted translation (CAT) tools, which are mainly fairly pricey proprietary programs (some free and open-source programs are available)

- A website (see the marketing chapter for details) with an associated e-mail address

- Business cards

- Dictionaries on CD-ROM and print editions

- Membership(s) to professional organization(s)

- Annual fees, such as business licenses

- A home office or leased/virtual office space

- Marketing materials, including brochures, professional photos, etc.

- Funds for traveling to professional development events, such as conferences and workshops

This list is not exhaustive by any stretch of the imagination, and is simply meant as food for thought. You should create your own list and decide what the basics are to you. Then you can use that list as the basis for the essential items. If there is something you would like to buy that it is not on your personal list, than it is probably not essential to running your business. That said, this does not mean that you do not need it or should not have it, but it just means that it falls in the beyond-the-basics category. When trying to decrease your expenses, keep this list in mind to help you refocus on how many expenses you can strip away without affecting the operation of your business. It is quite amazing how little is needed to run our businesses, which is one of the most tempting aspects of running a freelance translation business: there are very few overhead costs, so most of your income (minus taxes) will be profit. However, even when business is booming, you should evaluate your expenses and decide what is necessary and what is not.

Where to save

Even if your spending is modest, there are always ways to decrease it. Start by thinking of all your expenses – or better yet, look at your spreadsheet and ask yourself these questions: which of these items do I really need? Start distinguishing between needs and wants. For the time being, limit your expenses to the absolutely essential. You can always increase your expenses later, but decreasing them once they are higher can be a challenge. Save yourself the headache and do not even get used to spending more. And forget about what high-end things your colleagues and friends might have or use: you do not need to keep up with the Joneses, but your goal is to run a profitable, successful business.

Office supplies

If you are like most freelance linguists, your office supply expenses are probably quite minimal. However, there are always ways you can reduce your expenses.

Ink

For most translators, proofing final versions of projects on hard-copy paper is paramount. It is quite surprising how many mistakes one catches in print as opposed to just looking at a screen. In that sense, it is quite difficult to get around printing. An alternative would be to increase the font size to 150% or 200%, which will make proofing on your screen much easier. If you do print all your projects and spend quite a bit of money on ink, you need to think of ways of decreasing that cost. It sure is convenient when your manufacturer's site automatically gives you a pop-up telling you that you are low on ink and should re-order with one click, and this does save time and money by being quick and simple and not requiring a separate trip to a store. However, if you can save 30% by looking at alternative ways of buying ink, it is worth the little bit of extra time you will spend on it.

- **Refilling ink cartridges**: Many stores, from Walgreens to OfficeDepot, now offer refilling services for your used cartridges. This is not only budget-friendly, but also environmentally friendly.

- **Ordering on E-Bay**: For most models, you will find deals on up to 30% off on new and refurbished ink cartridges. You will have to pay for shipping and handling, but you will have to pay that if you bought the cartridges from the manufacturer's website as well. As a general rule, order online from trusted vendors who have excellent customer reviews and ratings.

- **Buy from discount online stores**. These sites offer machine-specific ink cartridges, both new and refurbished, many times at a significant discount. Depending on the size of the order, you might qualify for free shipping.

- **Ecofont**. This innovative company offers several fee-based packages of special fonts that you can install on your computer. The technology is quite fascinating, and when you print documents that use the ecofont, you save up to 25% on ink. Ecofont does offer one free, open-source font that you can download free of charge (http://www.ecofont.com).

- Not all ink cartridges are refillable, and not all refilled ink cartridges will work as well as manufacturer-made cartridges. If you are in the market for a new printer, consider verifying that the printer's cartridges can be refilled.

Paper

For both saving the planet and saving your budget, try printing on both sides of the paper, especially when you are just proofing your documents at home. If you send an actual hard copy to a client (which most of us rarely do, with the exception of certified translations), you need to print it out on nice, new paper. You might also consider purchasing recycled paper, which can actually be less expensive than the non-recycled variety. Another paper-saving alternative is to print multiple pages on one page. Depending on the size of the font and the layout of the document, this might be hard on your eyes, but it is worth a try.

Buy in bulk

If possible, join a members-only warehouse club, where you will be able to buy lots of business-related items at significant discounts over retail prices. Our favorite is Costco (www.costco.com). The business membership currently costs $50, which is a worthwhile investment in your business. Buying in bulk always pays off, especially if you are purchasing office supplies such as paper, ink, computers and accessories, pens, and filing folders. You can also buy office chairs, desks, and other bigger items.

Gadgets

For this category of expenses, you need to really take a hard look at wants versus needs. For instance, the iPhone is, without doubt, a fantastic gadget, highly functional and also very cool and hip. Before you decide to get any high-tech wireless device, such as a Blackberry, iPhone, or similar smart phone, think about how much business use you will get out of the device. Will you really respond to client inquiries from your phone? Can you afford a data plan for your company cell phone? Is the convenience of a smart phone worth the price?

Business phone and cellular phone

At the very least, you should have a dedicated business phone line, or at least one that you always answer as if it were strictly a business phone ("Good afternoon, thank you for calling The Spanish Wizards, this is Alejandra"). A very inexpensive option is calling your local phone provider and simply getting a different ringtone for business calls. However, you must be sure that the voice mail does not have your private message on it. After all, you are running a business and you must behave accordingly at all times, even if you work out of your house. Try to keep your personal and business phone separate and get your own business phone line if possible. In our case, we initially simply chose an online service, CallWave (www.callwave.com) that allows callers to go straight to an online voicemail for less than $10 a month with no actual phone. Then we would just use our home phone to call clients back. This worked well as long as the vast majority of potential clients contacted us online. As our business grew, we realized that we needed an actual phone number, and decided to cancel the service and get a dedicated business cellular phone.

Cellular services now run the gamut from free phone with contract to free phone with no contract and cheap phone with a special chip for only a certain carrier, and many more. It can be challenging to sort through all the different options and plans, because it is difficult to compare these non-standardized options. Whichever plan you choose to go with, opt for one that gives you flexibility in terms of changing your plan if your needs change. Sign up for a small-business plan, because these often offer significant advantages over personal plans.

Decrease the minutes if you are not using them. Your handy monthly bill will break down how many minutes you are really using. Most providers will let you switch your plan monthly if you would like. You might be surprised how few minutes you are using – we recently cut our minutes in half when we took a hard look at our cellular minute usage, and have not missed any of those minutes.

Alternative phone options

Going through the local landline phone company can sometimes be much pricier than you would think. Last year, we looked at the phone costs for the American side of our business and were quite surprised that they were exceeding $50 a month, which included $12 a month for voicemail. We quickly identified this as a great place to save money and looked for alternate options. Here are a few:

&. **Skype**: Most of us have heard of Skype (www.skype.com), the popular VoIP phone system (Voice over Internet Protocol), also known as internet phone or broadband phone. Basically, this term refers to technologies that transmit voice data over IP systems such as the internet. All you need is a computer and a headset with an integrated microphone. Skype is largely free, with all calls between Skype users completely free of charge. You have to sign up and install the free software to start adding people to your contact list (you can also directly call folks who are not in your contact list). Skype offers a great marketing opportunity, as you can add a picture, a link to your company, and even a permanent status message to your profile. With Skype, you can make calls to non-Skype users around the world for a very low cost. Skype's sound quality can, at times, be a bit shaky. While Skype is a great software program, we would not recommend relying exclusively on Skype for your business calls, as not all customers use Skype.

&. **Vonage**: We switched the American side of our business from our local cable service and phone provider to Vonage (www.vonage.com) and are happy with the $25/month savings and the excellent sound quality. Vonage is also a VoIP system, but it uses your existing phone line (the number will be transferred automatically once you sign up). You need to order a special adapter that you have to install on your computer (very simple, comes with color-coded non-techie instructions), which, depending on the model you choose, is available for a small fee (we chose the free one). The most popular plan is the one that offers unlimited domestic minutes, and Vonage also offers great international plans and rates. After you have set everything up, Vonage works just like a traditional phone. Only caveat: emergency calls to

911 work differently on Vonage, and the company goes to great lengths to tell you how it works. One of our favorite Vonage features is that it sends you an e-mail when you have received a message. If you are away from your desk, you can check the message remotely, and voicemail is included.

❧ **Jajah** (http://jajah.com) is a service based in Europe that we discovered a few years ago. It is also VoIP-based, analogous to Skype, and our favorite feature is that you can use your existing landline phone or even cellular phone. A set amount of minutes are free between Jajah users. Other calls, especially international calls, are very inexpensive, in the single-digit cent range for landline calls to certain countries. Jajah works on a pre-paid basis; and you can load money into your account with your credit card, which eliminates a bill at the end of the month. If you check the "add funds automatically" box, your account will be charged for whatever predetermined amount you chose to pay the previous time when your credit gets low.

Instant messaging

An informal phone service alternative is instant messaging. While we do not recommend it for formal communication with clients – unless it is at the client's request – it is a fantastic tool for communicating with colleagues. There are several free services you can use for this, including Skype (which, however, only lets you communicate with folks who also have Skype).

❧ **Gmail**. You can sign up for a free e-mail account at www.gmail.com, which undeniably has the best web-based e-mail interface available today. It is clean, simple, and very user-friendly. We do not advocate using a free e-mail address as your business e-mail, but Gmail has a good instant messenger feature. If you are chatting with clients, the conversation will be saved, and you will have it for future reference if needed.

❧ **Yahoo**. Analogous to Gmail, you can get Yahoo chat for free when signing up for a free Yahoo e-mail account. The interface is similar and easy. Get started at http://messenger.yahoo.com/.

❧ **AOL instant messenger (AIM)**. AOL is one of the most popular instant messenger services. You will also need a free e-mail account with AOL to get the free chat system. You can categorize your online contacts by groups (i.e., clients, friends, colleagues). Download the free software at http://www.aim.com/aimexpress.adp.

Trillian. When you start using instant messaging, you will soon realize that your contacts use many of the different clients describe above, which are generally not able to talk to each other. This means that if one of your clients is on Yahoo and you are on AOL, you will not be able to have a conversation via instant messenger. However, there is a nifty free tool called Trillian, which is not only very secure but also lets you talk between MSN Messenger, AIM, and others (not Gmail). It allows you to combine all your contacts, regardless of the system they use. Download it for free at http://www.ceruleanstudios.com/

Postage

Sooner or later, you will need to purchase stamps, even though you might be handling most of your invoicing and other written correspondence via e-mail. While invoices sent by mail do look more professional, most clients seem to be quite content with electronic invoices. The best way to purchase stamps in the U.S. is to get forever stamps that will not expire if the postage rates increase. If you can, buy these stamps in bulk, at places like Costco, where the stamps are sold below their face value. In many countries around the world, you can even have personalized stamps made with your company logo at a relatively affordable price.

Coupons are your friend

Perhaps you think that it is not worth your time – think again. If you can get $5 off for a few minutes of your time, it is very well worth it. However, always do a quick cost-benefit analysis. If it takes you two hours to find a coupon that will save you $10, that is not the best use of your time. A good option is signing up for in-store cards. For instance, at OfficeDepot, where we get much of our higher-quantity printing done, we signed up for the frequent purchaser card for small businesses. We have received several coupons, including a $20 rewards certificate for items purchased the previous quarter.

The library is your friend

The local library is a great resource not only for your professional life, but also for your personal life. We are constantly keeping our languages fresh by reading as much foreign-language literature as possible. While we are serious bibliophiles and truly enjoy owning many books, the cost-saving advantage of getting books from the library is significant. In addition, we get a good selection of business and travel books from the library. Your local library is also an inexpensive source for foreign films to keep you up-to-date with what is going on in your source or target language.

What not to save on

As much as we like saving money, there are a few things that, as an entrepreneur, you should not skimp on. Here is a non-exhaustive list of items that are worth the investment:

- A good office chair

- An ergonomic desk

- A good desktop or laptop computer

- Anything that will help prevent carpal tunnel syndrome: ergonomic wireless mouse, wrist rests, etc.

One of your main goals should be to stay healthy so you can continue running your business. Repetitive stress injuries are very common in our line of business, so try to prevent them as much as possible. In addition, some other things are certainly worth the investment in your long-term health, such as occasional massages (ask for them as birthday gifts!) to loosen up tight shoulder and arm muscles, a gym membership, or simply your time: take it and go for a walk. Get your eyes away from the computer and breathe some fresh air. Getting up every hour or so to do a few stretches or simply averting your eyes from the computer for a few minutes is also a good idea. For more health and happiness tips, please see our work/life balance chapter.

DEAR MS. PAM,
I AM AFRAID I CANNOT ACCEPT THE LAST ASSIGNMENT BECAUSE OF PERSONAL ETHICAL REASONS.

ETHICAL REASONS? I NEVER UNDESTOOD WHAT THAT MEANS... IT'S JUST THE USER MANUAL FOR SOME WEAPONS. HELPING TO DEFEND YOUR OWN COUNTRY IS A NOBLE TASK.

THE MANUAL IS ABOUT ANTI-PERSONNEL MINES DISGUISED AS TOYS! *THEY ARE TARGETED AT KIDS!!!!*

I'LL LOOK FOR ANOTHER, MORE PROFESSIONAL TRANSLATOR.
BESIDES THAT, I'M ALSO LOOKING FOR SOMEONE TO ACTUALLY TEST THE PRODUCT. DO YOU HAVE CHILDREN?

http://mox.ingenierotraductor.com

© 2009 Alejandro Moreno-Ramos

CHAPTER 3

≷⊛

SOCIAL MEDIA & WEB 2.0

A lot has changed since the internet was first introduced to the public in the mid-1990s. No longer do we just use the internet to browse pages created by someone else. With the advent of what is commonly referred to as web 2.0, the internet is much more interactive, making it easier than ever to keep up with news, to stay connected to friends, to share information, and to get to know new people.

According to Tim O'Reilly, who coined the phrase in 2004, "Web 2.0 is the business revolution in the computer industry caused by the move to the internet as a platform, and an attempt to understand the rules for success on that new platform."[1]

So what makes web 2.0 so special? Is it enough to just have a blog to be part of the new era? Does it simply mean that "old" websites have to be adapted and updated to conform to the newer look and feel of web 2.0 sites such as Flickr, or del.icio.us? It really does not mean that, and the underlying change goes far beyond the technological advancement in web technologies. In addition to that development, the web environment has fundamentally changed. Web 2.0 is based on the idea of collaboration.[2]

Social media, as a component of web 2.0, recognizes our desire to connect and interact with others, even if only on a virtual level. Web 2.0 is a very large field that includes communication tools such as blogs and social networks, collaborative tools such as opinion-sharing sites and wikis, multimedia (photo- and video-sharing), entertainment platforms and much, much more. In this chapter, we will focus on what is most useful for us as language professionals: blogging, micro-blogging, and social and professional networks such as Facebook and LinkedIn.

---

1   Cook, Niall (2008): Enterprise 2.0, page 12.
2   Gruber, Thomas, "Einsatzmöglichkeiten, Chancen und Nutzen von Web 2.0-Tools im Projekt-management" (German-language thesis, University of Vienna, Austria, 2009), page 12 – 13.

As fantastic as web 2.0 is, it goes without saying that you need to take everything with a grain of salt. Just like with printed media, just because it is published online does not mean that it is necessarily true. Rely on reliable and reputable sources.

Blogging

These days, almost everyone has one – a blog (short for weblog). Some are more interesting than others, and the vast majority of personal blogs are of no great benefit to anyone but the writer, which is perfectly legitimate. The internet is a big place with lots of space for anyone to write about anything. There are blogs for parents who want to bring up bilingual children, blogs of folks documenting wildlife in their backyards, musings about the best cocktail on Bora Bora, high school students exchanging test strategies, and very narrow subject matters (fine-tuning Bösendorfer pianos, and analysis of grass types in South African wilderness areas, just to name a few). In addition to personal-type blogs, which mostly chronicle what happens in one's personal life, the second form of blogging is professional blogging. There are millions of professional blogs on the blogosphere, covering everything from (you guessed it) web 2.0, sports, politics, marketing, religion, entertainment, restaurants, travel, parenting, cars, real estate and woodworking to antique toy trains. You name the most obscure subject you can think of, and there will be a blog, or hundreds, on the topic. For our profession, some of the most interesting blogs usually focus on translation, the business of translation, life in translation, technology for translators, dealing with difficult business situations, etc. There are many fantastic translation blogs that can provide excellent food for thought for your colleagues, and the exchange of information can really be invaluable.

While we have run several language-related blogs for years, we started our main translation blog, Translation Times (www.translationtimes.com) in 2008, at the urging of some of our talented colleagues who were already blogging themselves. We were initially a bit skeptical about adding another blog to our blogload (we write a German literature blog, a German translation mistakes blog, an English-language food blog, a German-language short story blog, and a German ortography blog), but it has been a fantastic experience.

Benefits of having a blog

A blog is a great way to share your insights into the business and to communicate news and interesting tidbits to colleagues and the general public. It can be a good tool for establishing credibility in the field. While it is not a direct marketing tool, successful blogs usually have quite a bit of "linking power" to the bloggers' business site via the link in the "About Us" section or in the footer. Do not directly promote your business too much on your blog – having the link is enough, and focus on high-quality content that is relevant to your readers. While you have a business to run, a blog should not be used as a direct way of advertising because you will lose readers very quickly. Readers stick to reading their favorite blogs because they provide updated, relevant information. High-quality entries and posts are the way to build readership, and you must keep this in mind when setting out to write posts. Blogs usually index fairly high on search engines, so if someone searches for you by name, chances are that your blog will come up high in the search results. Hence, you have to be very careful what you write about – it is very likely that potential customers will see it. On the other hand, you do not have to engage in self-censorship and refrain from writing what is on your mind. Just keep a good balance of posts that are highly relevant to your readers. If you do want to vent about something, make sure there is an angle that is of interest to others. For instance, we recently posted a warning about a non-paying customer on our blog, and we mentioned the company's name. We checked on this with an attorney friend, and he assured us it was not libel, as we just stated the obvious: that the company had not paid us for our services. We also shared this information on several translation sites where one can leave information about non-paying customers, among them, the very useful Payment Practices (membership-based, www.paymentpractices.net), but wanted to make this information available for all our colleagues around the world who might not subscribe to any of these services. To our complete surprise and delight, a translator contacted us via e-mail saying that he was based in Florida and that he would be more than happy to try to collect the money on our behalf. He even volunteered to drive to the non-paying customer's office and wait on their doorstep – we were stunned by so much collegial outpouring.

Another reason for having a blog is that you can share some personal information with your colleagues and get to know them better in an informal way. We have learned a lot about our colleagues by reading their blogs, where they have let us in on what frustrates them, how they work, and which translation rituals they have. It has been quite fascinating to embark on this blogging journey. Another advantage of blogging is that you are getting your name out in cyberspace in a way that you can fully control, since you are the one writing the articles and clicking on "publish." Getting your name associated with well-written, useful information is a good thing for your reputation in the marketplace and for your reputation with potential customers. You never know: your hard work on the blog may lead to some business. Be aware that these blog entries will most likely be around online for a long time. Even after you delete entries from your blog, they will remain in cyberspace and will be accessible through such sites such as www.archive.org.

Should you have a blog?

You should consider it, as long as you can make a commitment to publishing new, fresh, and interesting content at least once a week, which initially sounds like a daunting task. However, entries should be quite short, hence catering to users' short online attention span, which is well-documented by research into online reading habits. Ted Selker of the Massachusetts Institute of Technology recommends: "Give yourself a question, give yourself a goal, write it down. Follow that goal, know why you are surfing."[3] As a blogger, you need to keep these reading habits in mind to ensure that your audience reads what you have to say. To keep things short and interesting, you can simply post a link to someone else's blog commenting that you really enjoyed a specific article and want to share it with the rest of the blogosphere. Once in a while, we link to a funny, high-profile translation mistake (sometimes it is a video), a task we usually reserve for Fridays. This kind of post does not take a lot of time. The editorial-style entries take a bit longer, so we limit them to a few a month. Many times, we post about new dictionaries, new free and open-source software, and other tools and gadgets that make our lives as freelance translators easier. We will post links to interesting seminars and conferences worldwide and do the occasional book or dictionary review. If you are passionate about your industry and your profession and think you can communicate that knowledge to your readers, then a translation-related blog is for you.

Remember that if you decide to write a blog, it needs to be grammatically and stylistically impeccable. While blogs on other topics might have some leeway – actually, some technology blogs are clearly not written by writers – but as a language professional, you have to live up to a higher standard. Potential clients will hopefully visit your blog, and as it might be your very first impression of your writing abilities, you need to vow them. As tempting as it is to quickly draft a blog posting and make it live to the world without proofing it, please resist the temptation. Every piece of writing, whether it is a translation or a blog entry, that leaves your desk should be thoroughly proofed and edited. Very good linguists are traditionally exceptional writers, and your blog needs to reflect that.

Blogging platforms

By far, Wordpress (http://wordpress.com) and Blogger (https://www.blogger.com/start) are the most commonly used blogging platforms, so we will focus on them exclusively. They are both free of charge and you can get started very quickly and easily through a simple registration process.

The two platforms are quite similar. We started with Blogger, as it is the easier of the two, but have since created several blogs with Wordpress, which is significantly more flexible and has the ability to integrate with many plug-ins to

3   http://news.bbc.co.uk/2/hi/science/nature/1834682.stm

enable your blog to do more. Both Blogger and Wordpress are template-based, which means that you need absolutely no programming skills to create your blog. You simply select options, colors, backgrounds, layouts, etc. Wordpress has more options than Blogger, but is a little bit more involved in terms of creation. Our advice is to read up on both platforms and decide which one you feel comfortable with. If you want to keep things nice and simple, go with Blogger. If you like the thought of constantly adding new items, such as plug-ins, and like the flexibility of a myriad of templates, we recommend you use Wordpress.

Blog hosting options

There are two ways to host a blog: to host your own (self-host) or to have a hosted blog.

&. **Hosted blogs**: When your blog is "hosted," it simply means that you do not own a domain name, which is reflected in the URL. It also means that all your content and data will sit on the server of the service that you are using to create and host your blog. The main downside is that it is a bit less professional-looking, because your URL will include the blogging platform. For instance, your URL would be http://yourblog.blogger.com or http://yourblog.wordpress.com. Another potential downside, although unlikely, is that you could, theoretically, lose all your content if Blogger or Wordpress decided to stop hosting your blog for whatever reason (it is at their discretion). This a remote possibility, but if it happens, you will have no control over the fate of your data. The main upside is that there are no costs whatsoever involved with maintaining and hosting your blog this way.

&. **Self-hosted blog:** With a self-hosted blog, all your content sits on the hosting account that you own. The main upside to this option is that your blog's URL is more professional, and you will have a "true" domain name; that is, without the blog platform in the name of the URL, as is the case with hosted blog. Your URL would be anything of your choosing, such as www.translationmatters.com. When it is self-hosted, your blog's content is published on our own domain, which is available for a low fee.

It is certainly true that you need a little bit more web expertise, including some knowledge of HTML, FTP and web server settings to self-host your blog, but this can be learned relatively quickly. Consider enlisting the help of a technology expert to help you with the basics should you need more assistance. Luckily, web space is quite inexpensive these days, and most hosting companies, which are the providers from whom you will buy web space and domain names, have excellent tutorials and great support to help you through the set-up process. If this all sounds a bit too intimidating, stick to a hosted blog or find a technology expert to help you with the set-up of the web space, the domain, and to guide you through the process. Once it is set up, you will probably not need any additional help.

&. **The cost:** Hosting your own blog involves some cost. All the hosted blogs are completely free. The cost for web space is quite affordable at roughly $5 - $10/month for hosting, while the domain will cost roughly $10 a year. The price for the domain name will depend on the domain. For instance, a .com domain is usually more expensive than .net or a country-specific domain such as .de, .us, etc. In total, you will be spending roughly $100 per year for hosting your own blog on your own web space (be sure to log this as a business expense). Most hosting providers let you add more than one domain to your web space. This means that if you decide to add a second blog, or even a website, you would only have to pay the yearly domain name fees not and not another 12 months of webhosting fees. There are many reliable web space providers. We recommend Bluehost (www. bluehost.com), as they offer excellent prices and solid support.

RSS feeds

Readers will have a chance to sign up for your RSS feeds, which means that your latest blog entries will be added to the reader's personalized homepages (such as iGoogle, Netvibes or others[4]) to their bookmarks. RSS feed stands for "Really Simple Syndication" and is a family of web feed formats in a standardized format that are used to publish information that is updated frequently, such as news sites and blogs. Simply put: your readers will not have to remember to visit your blog, as their start page or bookmarks will immediately tell them if you have added a new entry to your blog. RSS feeds are an excellent way to make following your blog easy for your readers, and we recommend you encourage people to subscribe to yours. The way to do this is to add an "RSS feed" button to your blog. This is easily done through your blog hosting service. All you have to do is look under options or settings, depending on the service you use. Be sure to place the button in a prominent place on your blog so people can easily find it. It is quite frustrating to find a blog that you like and then being unable to locate the RSS feed button.

Another good aspect of RSS feeds is that they will enable you to save time, as RSS feeds make it possible to write a piece of content only one time and then publish it on various web 2.0 platforms, which all speak the same RSS language. Hence, the information can be interchanged and you can achieve more with less work.

---

4   http://mashable.com/2007/06/29/personalized-homepages/

About Me

The About Me/About Us/About section is an essential part of your blog, and you should spend some time writing good content about who you are and what you do. Include a recent image of yourself and the written version of the so-called elevator pitch. More than likely, the "About Me/About Us" page is the very first page that any new reader will see and focus on when visiting your blog, so you will have a few moments to catch the reader's attention (remember the short attention spans of online readers?) and to get interested in your blog. Share who you are, what your business is, what your goals are, your contact information, and any other relevant information[5]. Resist the urge to share your life story, but make your story stand out and memorable. We have seen some excellent About sections, including a web designer who put his face on Mount Rushmore, About Me pages with highly artistic elements, and very minimalist pages.[6]

Blogging food for thought

Here are 10 things you need to know if you are thinking about starting a blog.

*   **The technology is simple and easy to learn.** We know that sometimes it is not easy to learn new technologies and software. However, rest assured that learning how to blog is very simple. There is only a very shallow learning curve involved in working with either Blogger or Wordpress. You do not need any programming or layout skills. All the templates are pre-programmed, so you just plug in your text and you are ready to go.

*   **Typos and mistakes can be fixed.** The beauty of the internet is that you can fix any typos that you might have made, so relax. If you make a typo, fix it. While you should be very careful with grammar and spelling to give your blog the professional look and feel that it deserves, everything is changeable.

*   **It will take some time to build readership**. Readers might not immediately read and follow your blog. It will take time for your colleagues to hear about your blog and become interested in it, so do not be discouraged if there are not lot of people visiting your blog in the first few months (you can sign up for free activity reports with Google Analytics). It might seem like you are writing only for yourself in the beginning, but that is not the case. Good things will happen if you keep on writing.

---

5   http://www.bloggingbasics101.com/2009/08/how-do-i-write-an-about-me-page/
6   http://www.smashingmagazine.com/2009/07/01/best-practices-for-effective-design-of-about-us-pages/

Images. Including images makes blog postings that much more interesting and enjoyable. Make absolutely sure that you either own the copyright to the image or that the image is available for free in the public domain. You should not compromise your ethical standards here, so give credit where credit is due. If you are using someone else's image, you need to ask for permission to publish it first. The easiest way for us to use images is to use photos that we have taken ourselves whenever it is appropriate or relevant.

It will take up some of your time. While there are no hard rules on how often you should post, you should post regularly. We post roughly twice a week, and average about eight to 11 monthly postings on our translation blog, Translation Times (www.translationtimes.com).

Your blog will increase your online visibility. Having a blog makes it much easier for potential customers to find out about you. This is a good thing, and infinitely cheaper than buying an ad anywhere. Even though everyone knows that blogging is free and that it does not necessarily mean that your professional services are outstanding, it does show a level of commitment and professionalism that is difficult to ignore. You can also link to your blog from your homepage, which lets visitors click on the "blog" section to read your insight into the language services world.

Surround yourself with good people. You can decide to have a "blog-roll," which is essentially a set of links to other people's blogs. Choose carefully and link only to relevant blogs that your readers might enjoy. This means that you should follow these blogs for a while before you link to them.

Not everyone will agree with you. If you would like, you can let readers participate in the conversation by allowing them to leave comments (see the "dealing with comments" section for more details). Be prepared for fellow professionals to disagree, which usually results in interesting discussions.

Think like a blogger. Once you start writing a blog, you will constantly be looking for interesting bits of information that you can share with your colleagues, which is a lot of fun. It is analogous to seeing the world through a photographer's eye – you have a different focus and spend time thinking about your next blog posting wherever you are. Many times, we find inspiration in the print media, in something that has happened in our business, or in something that we heard about from a colleague. If we think it is of interest to others, we will share it.

&. Find ways to be interesting. It will come as no surprise that there are millions of blogs clogging up cyberspace. Luckily for language blogs, there are relatively few focused specifically on translation and interpretation in a specific language, certainly not more than a few hundred (that we know of) that are updated regularly. Even with a relatively small amount of competition, you need to stand out from the crowd if you would like to grow your readership. Write compelling articles with good images, even if it takes longer. Put thought into what you have to say, even if it might be controversial, and report important language-related news. Being the first to report something will undoubtedly make your blog interesting.

How much time should I spend on it?

The beauty of blogging is that you can spend as much or as little time on it as you want. The way to build readership and to keep your readers engaged is to produce new content on a regular basis, ideally, several times a week. However, there is no magic rule: perhaps all you can commit to is posting once a week, which is fine. It is important to be fairly consistent in your postings. We regularly stop following blogs if they do not produce new content on a regular basis or we see that there have not been any new postings in more than a month. After all, we follow blogs because we want to learn something and exchange ideas, and that can only be done with fellow bloggers who also put the time and effort into keeping their blogs going. Do not let the need for routinely updated information discourage you: you do not have to write 500 words for every entry: quite the contrary. According to analytics software that we use to get anonymous information on how many visitors read our blog, the average visitor spends roughly one minute and thirty seconds reading our blog. Quick posts in the 100-200 word range are just fine, and you can write longer articles as you see fit. While your writing might be quite sophisticated and eloquent, this is not the place to show off your literary skills. It is best to simply and quickly formulate what you have to communicate and point the reader to further information if they would like to read more. A good idea for blogging is to work ahead when you have some free time and create as many blog posts as you want and save them as drafts. Then, whenever you are ready – it can be when you are really busy – all you have to do is hit the "publish" button and your blog posting will be live to the world. When we have a slow day, as we all invariably do, we use the time to write dozens of postings that we have been meaning to write. That way, even when we are really busy, we are still posting fresh content on our blogs.

What kinds of blog postings should I put up?

When we first started blogging, we were in awe of all the amazing content our peers were producing on their blogs, and wondered if we would ever be able to do the same thing. Quite honestly, we were a bit intimidated by the wealth of information and asked ourselves: do we have information to share on a consistent basis that will be of interest to others? After several years, we can answer that question in the affirmative. Here are some things you can post about.

Opinion pieces. Do you have something to say? Is there something that has been bothering you? Something positive or negative? Say it here. Feel free to let your hair down a bit, but keep in mind that whatever you write will reflect on you and potentially your business. This does not mean you should sugar-coat everything you write, but should serve as a reminder that this is not a diary. You have no obligation towards unbiased reporting – quite the contrary – but for others' reading pleasure, consider trying to present both sides of the story.

Advice pieces. Did you recently learn about something that you want to share with others? How about making it a regular feature on your blog? It could be called "New software of the month" or "Business development 101." Fellow professionals love hearing about what others are learning, and sharing what we know makes for a stronger languages community.

Links to other blogs. Did you read something interesting on another writer's blog? Consider linking to it. You can preface your posting by saying that you really enjoyed this particular blog posting and then provide the link to it.

Guest post blogs. Invite fellow professionals – linguists or others – to contribute to your blog. You could ask to have a guest post by someone whose blog you follow and that you like. Ideally, you will have engaged in a conversation with the other blogger through comments or e-mail. Suggest an ideal length and a topic that you have in mind (perhaps the bloggers' main expertise), and kindly ask for their help. You will be providing a link back to the guest blogger's own blog and provide a quick bio and an image.

- **Links to other blogs where you are a guest blogger.** Similarly, you can be a guest blogger on other people's blogs. While you may certainly approach other blogs about providing a guest post, it is better to wait until you get invited. Give your blog some time to be read and recognized, and do not expect to be a guest blogger within your first few months of blogging. You have to build your blogging reputation and give others the chance to follow your blog for a while.

- **Postings about upcoming professional development opportunities.** We have learned about some great conferences through other blogs, and a blog is a fantastic way to spread the word about professional development seminars and conferences, which are largely put on by volunteers and deserve our support and public relations efforts.

- **News about the translation industry.** This might include information that you have received from colleagues who do not blog, information from listservs (e-mail lists) that you subscribe to, etc. If you think it is interesting, share it. Be sure to credit the original source. For instance, when we heard about the passing of a past president of the American Translators Association, we posted an "in memoriam" note with the limited information that was available at the time.

- **Postings about new technology solutions for translators.** Some colleagues probably do not spend as much time online as others, so if you find a great piece of technology, let others know about it. It is quite a challenge to keep up with developments in the software market, especially for translation memory tools, so we always enjoy hearing about nifty tools from others.

- **Reviews of books or dictionaries.** Do you have a favorite dictionary or online resource that you cannot live without? Write a quick review about it and tell your readers where to buy or access it.

- **Anecdotes from your business life.** The good, the bad, and the ugly – why not share it in a tasteful and professional way? Did your pet iguana unplug the computer by mistake? Was your notary unavailable when you needed a notarized translation? Did you just get a fantastic compliment from your favorite client that had you smiling for a week? Blog about it.

&. **The lighter side of translation.** This includes funny things related to our industry. You could post an interesting, funny tidbit, such as a translation gone wrong in the mainstream media, a funny printed translation mistake, or a relevant cartoon. It might not be funny to everyone, but that is not the goal. We recently posted a video of the Miss Universe 2009 pageant, where the contestants' interpreter committed some serious mistakes, which was good food for thought for interpreters.

&. **Surveys/polls.** This is a great way to engage the audience. Why not take a quick poll (free, simple, polling software is available for this) and get to know your readers better? You could ask how many people routinely work on the weekends, which operating systems they use, whether they work with agencies or direct clients, etc. Many readers are usually willing to participate in these surveys, and the results can be quite surprising.

&. **Get creative.** There are no rules or limits to what you can write about. The more you write, the easier it will get, and next thing you know, you will have many different blog entries forming in your head before you even have time to jot them down.

What kinds of blog postings should I refrain from putting up?

This is a very personal decision. We follow a number of interesting blogs that stick to a positive, upbeat note about our industry and rarely criticize anyone – customer or professional organization – in any way, shape or form. We also really like other blogs that offer a more unfiltered take on our business, including rants and raves about annoying projects, ill-behaving customers, and troubles with technology, which is quite entertaining to read. Personally, we quickly lose interest in the blogs we read if they turn into complaint fests. We certainly acknowledge that there are many challenges in our profession, and we report on those as well, but we try to keep a good balance between the negative and the positive.

Dealing with comments

You have several ways of controlling and managing the comments left on your blog. You can choose to moderate comments before they go live to your blog or have them go directly online without reviewing them. We like moderating comments before they go live, as we want to make sure there is no spam and that no one is saying anything offensive or is trying to promote their (unrelated) business. With both Wordpress and Blogger, we have the option to publish, reject or edit. It is surprising how many folks have tried to take advantage of all the hard work we have put into our blog by leaving comments along the lines of "Great entry! Check out my website at: www.becomingamillionaire.com". These kinds of comments go directly into the trash, as they provide no value to our readers. Translation blogs, as a general rule, should not be geared toward e-commerce and should be mostly informational. Of course, in the long run, some business opportunities may arise through your translation blog, but that should not be your first priority. Do not let others use your forum for self-promotion: if you are not promotiong your own services on your own blog, no one else should, either. Some blog owners also require the commenters to verify that they are human by typing in a string of letters and numbers, which is another good way to restrict spam.

Here is an overview of the options you have for dealing with comments.

Not accepting comments. You could not allow comments on your blog, which we do not think is a good solution. After all, part of the idea of your blog is to build readership and to get comments so you can engage in collegial exchange with your readers. Sometimes, the most interesting parts of a blog are the comments.

Publishing comments immediately. You can choose to have all comments that are left on your blog to be live immediately, which means that you will not be able to look at them first.

Moderating comments. This is our preferred option. We like to have a look at the comments before we publish them. 99% of the time, we publish them. With this option, after the person has left a comment, a message along the lines of "your comment is awaiting moderation" will be shown. The blog owner will then receive an e-mail message to whichever address was specified under the blog settings. That e-mail will contain a link and give you options to reject, publish, or moderate the comment.

Rejecting comments. A few comments might be completely inappropriate. Since it is your blog, you get to decide which criteria you want to use for rejecting comments. Will you reject it if someone completely disagrees with you? If they try to promote their own blog? If the comment does not contribute anything to the discussion? As a general rule, we only reject comments that attack or offend others who have commented previously, comments that are clearly spam and comments that use our platform to promote their services or their own blog without contributing anything to the topic.

Responding to comments. Many times, we engage in conversations with colleagues who leave comments, even if it just thanking them for their time and input. Our goal is to learn from others as well, so we like to keep the conversation going through the comments. Including different opinions and different ways of looking at issues is a good thing and it shows your readers that you have an open mind. We try to keep the tone of the blog and the comments positive, but we do not shy away from controversy and welcome all comments, whether they differ from our opinions or not.

Commenting on other blogs

One of the best ways of interacting with others is to leave relevant comments on their blogs. In general, we stay away from simply saying "great article" and only comment when we have something insightful to add to the topic at hand. When you leave a comment, you will have the chance to add a URL, and we usually provide our blog's URL. Whoever sees our comment and finds it to be interesting will be able to click on the hyperlink and go to our blog. Comments are a great way to communicate what you know about a subject that someone else has written about. Do not forget to observe netiquette (online etiquette) when leaving a comment. Some topics can be controversial, especially if they represent an author's opinion, and we cannot all agree on everything, which is good. This is the basis for intellectual debate and discussion. However, the comments section of a blog is not the place to get into heated arguments with the author or others who have left comments. And it is certainly not the place to be rude or disrespect other people's opinions, and it is not the right place to try to convince folks of your own opinion. While intellectual debate is a good thing, it should be engaged in with restraint, and perhaps moved to other channels once the exchange loses relevance for other readers.

When commenting on other blogs, be sure to use a Gravatar (Globally Recognized Avatar). Once you have registered it (a simple and quick process), your Gravatar, an image of your choosing, will follow you from site to site. Whenever you leave a comment on someone's blog and enter your name, your pre-chosen Gravatar will appear, hence customizing and personalizing your comment. Be sure to use a nice, professional-looking picture. Visit http://en.gravatar.com/ to get started.

Linking to other blogs

Consider adding a so-called blogroll section so your readers can discover other blogs that they might enjoy. When we first started our blog, we immediately linked to the blogs that inspired us to start our own writing. We then e-mailed the owners of these blogs and told them we had linked to them. We inquired whether they would be interested in linking to ours as well. Many were happy to do so right away, while others, rightfully so, wanted to follow our blog for a few months to see what kind of content we were developing. While you are not directly endorsing other people's content by linking to their blogs, you are giving them valuable space on your blog. In addition, we are partially defined by who our business associates are; so chose wisely. Our blogroll section is called "our favorite translation blogs and related sites." You can organize your blogroll in separate sections for translation blogs, translation associations, other translators' business sites, etc.

English-language translation blogs that we like

We regularly follow translation blogs in several languages, mainly in English. There are hundreds of excellent blogs, and we have compiled a short list of our favorite English-language blogs in no particular order. While new blogs are popping up relatively frequently, we are only listing blogs that have updated their content regularly for at least a year.

- **The GITS blog** (http://ginstrom.com/scribbles): Japanese->English software and telecommunications translator Ryan Ginstrom blogs about life as a translator in Japan, programming, and other things. Highly interesting perspectives from an overseas market.

- **Translate This!** (http://www.blog.wahlster.net): Michael Wahlster, an English->German electronics and telecommunications translator based in southern California, runs one of the oldest and best translation blogs. Michael's posts are short, easy to read, witty, and relevant.

- **Thoughts on Translation** (http://thoughtsontranslation.com): Colorado-based French->English translator and author Corinne McKay offer a wide array of useful, well-researched and beautifully written advice for linguists of all skill levels.

- **Speaking of Translation** (http://speakingoftranslation.com): Corinne McKay and her colleague Eve Bodeux created the first-ever podcast focused exclusively on translation. The episodes are free to listen to and to download and are full of important information and great interviews.

- **Mox's Blog (http://mox.ingenierotraductor.com/):** Alejandro Moreno-Ramos, an English/French to Spanish translator based in Spain, who is also the illustrator of this book, publishes hilarious cartoons about the world of translation and interpretation. Follow Mox and his friends and read about their weekly adventures.

- **The Wor(l)d-Weary Translator** (http://tomellett.blogspot.com): Tom Ellet, a Norwegian/German/Swedish to English translator in the Niagara region of Canada, writes about language, writing, and translation. Tom always has good points to make and insightful opinions to share.

🔖 **Say What!** (http://cinoche5.wordpress.com): Alexander Totz, a French<->English audiovisual translator and writer with a very interesting specialization blogs about the French and American film industry, subtitling, audiovisual translation, and more.

🔖 **Musings From an Overworked Translator** (http://translationmusings.com/): German->English translator Jill Sommers addresses issues in her busy translation practice, and writes, with humor and style, about business topics while giving lots of practical advice plus Friday funnies.

🔖 **There's Something About Translation** (http://www.dillonslattery.com): Sarah Dillon, a multilingual translator who lives in Australia, runs one of the most professional-looking and interesting blogs on translation, with a strong focus on web 2.0 and social media.

🔖 **About Translation** (http://aboutranslation.blogspot.com): Multilingual Colorado-based translator Riccardo Schiaffino, who also teaches translation, offers solid opinions, well-written articles, and interesting anecdotes. About Translation is one of the longest-running translation blogs, and Riccardo's posts are always smart and entertaining.

🔖 **Brave New Words** (http://brave-new-words.blogspot.com): B.J. Epstein, who holds a Ph.D. in translation, reports from the front lines of teaching and translating children's literature. Insightful and updated frequently. B.J. is a Chicago-born Swedish to English translator based in the U.K. who is constantly writing, translating, researching, teaching, or thinking about language.

🔖 **Translation Tribulations** (http://simmer-lossner.blogspot.com): German->English translator and technology expert Kevin Lossner dispenses highly useful tips and comments on his translation life from Germany. Kevin's posts are always spot-on and informative, and he is very gracious about sharing information with his colleagues.

Should I put ads on my blog?

We generally recommend against it. The amount of ads on websites sometimes seem to overpower the content, and many ads can be quite annoying (especially if they chirp, bounce, or flash). You do not want to create a blog that distracts the reader by placing irrelevant ads on the right-hand side. You could certainly sign up with Google Adsense and have text-only ads placed on your blog, but the money you can earn from this will be completely negligible unless you can attract more than a thousand users a day. A word of warning: surely you have heard of the self-proclaimed internet millionaires who live exclusively off the earnings of their blogs? While they do exist, there are very, very few of them. In order to earn just a few dollars, you are going to have to attract thousands of readers to your blog, which is an enormous challenge for a niche blog (this is infinitely easier if you are writing a blog about reality television). Our advice is to not waste your time and potentially alienate your readers in the process. The amount of money you are likely to earn from the ads will barely pay for your morning bagel – once a month, that is. A blog is not a money-making endeavor.

Microblogging services

Twitter, a microblogging tool, has only been around for a few years, and has already made quite a splash on the online social and professional media circuit. While its long-term business value may not be immediately apparent to skeptics, Twitter, along with other microblogging tools such as Pownce, Tumblr, and Jaiku[7], provides a very simple and quick way to expand the number of people who know about you and your services. For the sake of simplicity, we will focus on the web's most popular microblogging service: Twitter. At is very basic, Twitter is a tool that allows you to connect with ("follow" in Twitter-speak) people around the world who might be in your line of business or share some of your interests. Twitter, unlike Facebook and professional networking sites such as LinkedIn, has a very simple and clean interface and very few options on your profile page. It is easy to learn and only takes a few minutes to set up.

There are many benefits to being on Twitter, especially if you also write a blog, as you can easily cross-promote and help drive traffic to it. Twitter happens in real time, and you can use wonderful Twitter applications such as TweetDeck (www.tweetdeck.com) to sort through all the updates that are happening in your network (it also integrates with other platforms, such as LinkedIn and Facebook). The messages sent out through Twitter are known as "tweets." Twitter can also help you find new readers, is a great networking tool, and helps you keep your finger on the pulse of what is happening in both your industry and in others.[8]

---

7   http://www.readwriteweb.com/archives/10_micro-blogging_tools_compared.php
8   http://www.problogger.net/archives/2008/01/23/9-benefits-of-twitter-for-bloggers/

Say it in 140 characters or less

On Twitter, you have 140 characters to communicate anything you would like to: what you are working on, what you are thinking about, things you want to know by posting questions, asking for opinions, communicating what you have been up to, providing links to your blog and your website, responding to other's tweets, etc. One of the best ways to get followers on Twitter is to enter into meaningful dialogue with those in your network. This can include answering questions, offering insight, or retweeting others' tweets, which simply means passing on someone else's tweet to your followers, hence helping spreading the word. While it is certainly fine to mix business and personal tweets, avoid communicating too many trivial things. Rather, build a following by engaging your audience. Followers are the readers who have subscribed to your updates, and hence your updates will show up on the follower's Twitter feed. The number of followers is in the hundreds of thousands or even millions for certain Twitter superstars such as Richard Branson of Virgin Atlantic. Just like you would do with a blog, you achieve a large following by sharing interesting things, links to articles, links to blogs, pictures, video, etc. Alternatively, engage your followers by asking direct questions (Has anyone used the new Trados version? Has anyone run WordFast on Linux?) and thoughtfully answer questions that others might have. Post about things that are interesting to others, not only to you, and send your followers to relevant links. While many companies have made significant amounts of money on Twitter, such as Dell, which made $6.5 million from Twitter-related sales[9], that will most likely not be the case for you.

Be careful to not promote your services too aggressively, as followers will lose interest in you quickly if you do. Even if you cannot trace Twitter directly to sales, and chances are you will not, you can look at it as an easy-to-manage, free Yellow Pages of sorts. Do not forget to pay attention to your mini-profile, which will be displayed on the right-hand side of your publically visible Twitter page. Your mini-profile is what many potential followers will use as the information basis to decide whether you are worth following, so make the profile interesting and engaging. You can post one link to a website or blog and give a short overview (yes, 140 characters or less) of who you are and what you do. We recommend using your real name and a photo that you feel comfortable sharing with the world.

Following others

You should be following other peoples' updates as well, but you do not automatically have to follow everyone back who follows you (after all, this is not a link exchange game). Usually, when we get an e-mail telling us that someone is following us, we check out that person's profile, read their recent posts, and figure out whether what they have to say is interesting to us. If you want to follow the

9   http://www.bloomberg.com/apps/news?pid=newsarchive&sid=akXzD_6YNHCk

person, which means that their updates will appear on your page, you just click on "follow." We routinely choose not to follow people who say things like "social media superstar, turning your blog into money, online marketer, web 2.0 guru", because those profiles depict folks who are mainly on Twitter for sales purposes and do not produce relevant content. We prefer to follow colleagues, friends, linguists, and other professionals in other business or industries who have valuable things to contribute. We recently heard, via Twitter, that an international translation magazine was looking for contributors. We got the editor's information from our Twitter contact, and Judy is now a now regular contributor to that magazine. If it had not been for Twitter, we would not have known that the magazine was looking for more articles. It is a solid example of how Twitter works. One caveat: do not spend too much time on it. You could spend an eternity on Twitter, answering questions, reading other people's posts, clicking from Twitter to blogs to more blogs, engaging in conversations and chats by answering others' tweets until you reach the end of the internet. Be strict with yourself and limit yourself to a certain amount of time that you will be allocating to Twitter every day. We recommend sending out a few updates a day and spending 10-15 minutes reading your Twitter feed to see what is happening in the network. If you invest relatively little, you will not be disappointed if your investment does not result in any tangible outcome, but also remember that these are long-term investments in your network, your reputation, and your future.

Professional networks

Professional online networks have, in many ways, revolutionized the way that we look at our customers, clients, and co-workers. Now, all of a sudden, we have everyone's résumés at our fingertips. It is a very powerful to be connected to hundreds of thousands of people around the world. The basic idea behind online professional networks is a simple: it is networking, but online, where you never lose any business cards and can always find whom you are looking for without having to call a friend to say: "Remember this linguist we met a few months ago? This established legal translator, she works from Polish into Japanese; I think she lives in Portland and is a friend of Cindy Offenberg's?" Well, no more. The first thing one has to do is create a strong profile and then start building the network. Do not expect to have clients calling the first day you put up a professional profile. You should look at this more as a free way of getting professional information about yourself online that you control. Most professional profiles index very high on search engines, meaning that if a potential customer wants to know more about you and searches for your name, i.e., "Chelsea Gunters", your professional profile(s) will come up near the very top of the search results.

Top picks for professional networks

Our two favorite professional network sites are www.linkedin.com (the world's largest professional network with a strong U.S. focus; basic memberships are free, premium membership start at $24.95 per month) and www.xing.com (very large and significant as well, with its main focus on the European market, the basic membership is free, but the much more useful premium membership currently costs EUR 4.95 per month.) Since LinkedIn is by far the largest professional networking site on the internet, we will focus mostly on that site.

Professional networks 101

Here are a few good steps to follow when building your professional networks. The following tips are based on LinkedIn, but apply, in general, to all other professional online networks as well:

&. **Strong profile and job experience**: Basically, a profile can be based on your résumé, but it is much more sophisticated and interactive than a paper CV. Usually, the more information you enter, the better. Be truthful and honest, and describe your responsibilities for every position you have held. Highlight what you excel at and briefly describe your responsibilities. Just as with a paper CV, no one wants to read the equivalent of a novel, so make it short and interesting. Some linguists prefer to write about themselves in the third person, while many others stick to the first person. Either way is fine – just be consistent. After entering your most recent position (you do not have to fill out all the information at once, as you can always get back to it later), work your way back in time with your other work experience. A good idea is to also list any non-profits that you are currently working with, as those will also appear on the very top. For instance, you could say that you are the Treasurer of the Colorado Translators Association, which will appear as a real "job." The system allows you to have several jobs at the same time, as many of us do. While most of these positions at non-profits are volunteer positions, you should add them, as they round out your experience and show that you are committed to giving back to the community and take volunteer work seriously

&. **Picture**. You should, most definitely, include a professional picture of yourself. This does not mean you have to find a professional photographer and spend hundreds of dollars on headshots. Rather, it means that you should refrain from using a picture that was clearly taken for non-professional purposes: no sunglasses on your head, no snapshots, no pictures of you with other people clearly cropped out, no unbuttoned shirts or skimpy cocktail outfits. If in doubt, err on the side of the conservative.

Getting your network started. Some of the main benefits of online professional profiles is that you can create a network of people whom you know and trust, and hopefully, when you are trying to get introduced to someone like a potential client, you can find a contact in common (or second contact, or third). You will be surprised how many people you will be linked to through your contacts if you only have, say 50 contacts. The contacts grow exponentially, and maintaining and updating your profile is easy and free. We would suggest starting with current and past co-workers, as the system will automatically suggest these to you. The more past jobs you enter, the more suggestions for connections you will receive, as the system will query for people who have worked at the same companies that you have. However, remember that you should not connect to people just because you worked with them or they are a friend of a friend – choose wisely. Your group of peers and friends defines you, and this is no more apparent and important then on LinkedIn. As a general rule, it is a good idea not to accept connection invites (called "invitation to connect") on LinkedIn from people you do not know personally or who are not connected to at least one our your trusted contacts. Once in a while, have a look at your contacts' contacts to determine if you know any of those folks. If you do not, but would like to be introduced, you can request an introduction through your connection. In terms of information being public, you can search LinkedIn's directory for anyone you want, and you will be able to see the person's profile page. However, what you will not be able to see is the person's contact information. This you can only see for people you are connected to directly. If you are not, and you still want to contact him or her, you need to find someone who can make that introduction. In the old days, you would have to call or e-mail your friends to see who knew someone at a company you wanted to target. Today, web 2.0 is your friend, and you simply get on LinkedIn.

Expanding your network. There are many folks with more than 500 connections, and others who are happy just having a handful. Either scenario is fine, and the strategy you choose depends on what you would like to get out of the professional network. If you simply want your complete information and résumé to be easily visible and found by potential customers who search for you online, then having just a few connections is good enough for your purposes. However, if you would like to grow your business and want more people to know about your services, you need to be a bit more strategic. In theory, the more people know about your services, the better. Given that your customers can come from a variety of fields and businesses, you do not have to stick to just one group. Focus on expanding your network in your specialty or area of interest in conjunction with other related fields.

ba **Recommendations**. Most likely, you will have to ask for them. Ideally, folks would recommend you voluntarily, but that is not very likely. We are all busy people, and sometimes adding to someone else's résumé (or online profile, in this case) is not on the top of our priority list. So, in order to get recommended, you need to ask for it, even if it feels awkward and forced. Be sure to ask people whom you know well and who are very familiar with your abilities. It is good to have recommendations from a variety of people, including co-workers, former or current supervisors, former or current direct reports, and mentors or mentees. LinkedIn has an online interface where you can easily request a recommendation from a specific person, and you can also add a personal message. In many cases, your contact will ask you to recommend them back, which is fine. It is best if you receive recommendations by people whom you have not recommended, so it does not look like you are simply doing each other a favor.

ba **Groups**. Groups are a fantastic way to add to your online profile. They will be listed at the bottom of your profile under the heading "groups." You can choose to display the logo and the group's heading on your page. Some groups are members-only and require that you apply for free membership and be approved. There is a myriad of groups you can join; everything from your high school's alumni group and industry-specific associations to volunteer associations. We belong to language-specific associations, to translation and localization groups and to alumni groups from our universities and corporations where we have worked. You can choose to receive daily or weekly updates from activities of the group, which mainly consist of members posting questions and answers to each other. It is quite interesting to keep your finger on the pulse of the industries you work in. While there is no ideal number of groups to belong to, resist the temptation to belong to too many groups just for the sake of amassing them on your profile. Think quality, not quantity, and join the groups that are the most relevant to you and your areas of specialization.

Additional LinkedIn applications, status updates, and daily digest

LinkedIn has a variety of additional applications you can install and add to your profile. Here are a few:

ba **Upcoming trips**. Through the www.tripit.com application, you can easily and quickly add upcoming trips to your profile. These can be directly pulled from your travel purchases (airlines, major travel websites, etc.) if you add them to the distribution list of the confirmation e-mail. Alternatively, you can add the details of the trip manually. This is a very handy tool if you want your entire network to know where you are. It is almost equivalent to sending out an out-of-office message, and in many cases, we have heard via LinkedIn that one of our contacts will be in one of our cities and have been able to get together with that person. The application will also automatically tell you which of your contacts are in a given city (either permanently or traveling to it as well) during the time that you are there. This is a great tool – and has in the past, reminded of us acquaintances we needed to see when we were not aware that they were in a particular city. Again, keep in mind that LinkedIn indexes very high on search engines, so the more updates you make to your profile, the better. Fresh content, even if it is just a new trip, makes your profile more interesting.

Upcoming events. This is a handy tool for conferences and events. You can add upcoming events to your calendar, whether you are the organizer, an attendee, or a presenter. For instance, most translation organizations post their conferences on LinkedIn, so you can RSVP to them (with no obligation) and see who else is going. We frequently post about events that we are presenting at to keep others in the loop and to let our network know about our activities.

Slideshows. LinkedIn, through an application called Slideshare (www.slideshare.com), allows you to add slideshows to your profile. These come in handy if you have been presenting at a conference and want to share the slideshows with the attendees, many of whom will be on LinkedIn.

Update your status. Similar to the social networks, such as Facebook and Twitter, LinkedIn also lets you update your status and enter information about what you are doing, what you are working on, where you are traveling to, etc. Your contacts, who, just like you, can subscribe to daily or weekly updates, will see the changes you have made on your page. Many times, contacts have commented on our status, for instance, congratulating us on a seminar or a translation project we are working on, which has resulted in a nice professional dialogue.

Daily e-mail digest and the management thereof. Depending on your preferences, you can sign up to receive as much or as little information about what your contacts are doing on LinkedIn. Weekly digests are a good tool to see what is happening without getting too much e-mail. This way, you will find out who has switched jobs and who has left a company. You can use this as valuable information to fine-tune your marketing strategy: it is quite useful to know that one of your existing contacts just moved into a new position at a company you would like to have as a client. Use the information and consider dropping your contact a congratulatory message through LinkedIn or e-mail.

Social networks

As opposed to professional networks, social networks' main purpose is allowing you to keep up with the people in your personal life. While personal profiles are not exactly geared toward getting you business or promoting your services, they can still be great, free, promotional tools. As an entrepreneur, your personal life and your professional life will often overlap. Ours overlap all the time – we have friends who are customers and clients who are friends – so we use both professional and social networks to talk about what is happening in our professional lives. A few months ago, an old friend of ours contacted us through Facebook and she ended up becoming a client. She probably had our card somewhere, but seeing our profiles every day reminded her that we were translators and made her think of us when she was looking for someone to translate her website into German. Many linguists use Facebook strictly for personal purposes and are not friends with anyone who could also be a client. In our lives, those lines are much more fluid. Many of our clients like being connected to us through both professional and social networks, because that way they always have our updated information and do not have to go looking for a business card or an e-mail address. Sometimes, a status message you post about a translation you are working on might trigger a response from one of your contacts and may even lead to business in the future.

When it comes to deciding what to share and what to keep to yourself, our mantra is that we do not put anything up online – on social or professional networks or anything else – that we would not want to see printed in the newspaper (or, in the spirit of the times, online) the next morning. Use your good judgment.

Top pick for social network

We have evaluated and participated in many social networks, and Facebook (www.facebook.com), the world's largest social network with 350 million users in 2009, takes the top prize. Some of the reasons are:

> **It is free**. Free is good for small business owners. Facebook also offers business accounts, which have much more limited access than personal accounts. Our advice is to create your account under your real name. You do not have to have your business name appear on Facebook to be able to promote your services, and using your real name ensures that more people can find you.

> **It indexes very high on search engines** if someone is trying to find you (old friend, potential customer, etc.)

Most of your contacts will be on it. This is the beauty of it: you will be able to keep up with friends old and new all in one place. No more e-mailing individual vacation pictures to people.

Only your friends can see your pages and access your information. Facebook's settings default to "private." If you choose to do so, you can make your profile entirely public, which means that everyone can see it and leave comments, even if they are not friends with you. Few users choose that option, and we have set our settings to "private." The same applies to the pictures, videos, and links we post – they are only for our friends' eyes. When you put up a photo album, you can easily choose who should be see-ing the images – your friends only, friends of friends, everyone, etc.

It has a simple, clean interface. Facebook has a relatively simple inter-face, which the company is constantly improving, and you can put up your profile page in a matter of minutes. No HTML coding is required – if you can write e-mail, you can do Facebook. There are hundreds of additional applications you can install and games you can play with others online, vir-tual gifts you can send, petitions you can sign, causes you can support, etc. At the very beginning, keep it simple. Fill in as much information about yourself as you would like, and since your private and your professional life will often overlap, be sure to add links to your website and to your blog on your profile.

Groups. Just like on LinkedIn, you can join groups here, including professional associations. We belong to several entrepreneurship groups, and they have generated some interesting discussions and organized real-life meetings. Joining a few relevant groups and receiving the occasional e-mail (which you can easily opt out of) is a good idea.

Getting started on Facebook

Go to www.facebook.com. The registration process is quick and only takes a few minutes. All you need is an e-mail account and your date of birth.

Your settings. Through your settings, you control who can see your information. Most users choose to have their settings in such a way that only their approved friends can see their start page, their information page, their images, etc. We suggest you do the same, unless you want as many people as possible to see your information (which some businesses want). Once your settings are saved, people wanting to view your page will need to be approved by you. They will send you a so-called friend request, which will be delivered to the e-mail address you specified in the system. Some users have dedicated e-mail addresses just for their Facebook e-mail, which is not necessary for us. You will then have the option to accept, reject, or ignore the friend invitation. As a general rule, we prefer to be friends on Facebook almost exclusively with people we know in the real world, mainly friends but also a few acquaintances. You might choose to handle this differently, and connect to only the people you feel comfortable with. The strategy is completely up to you. This really is like real life – just because someone wants to be your friend does not mean you have to feel the same way.

🐾 **Status updates.** One of the main things you can post on Facebook is an update on what you are doing at the moment by answering the question "What's on your mind?" on the very top of your profile page. Remember that everyone in your network (and your network's networks, if you so choose) will see what you post and will have the ability to comment on it. Many linguists frequently post about mundane things ("Eating an ice cream sandwich," "About to go to lunch," "At the gym") to very profound things like ("Wondering what can be done to reform America's health care system," "Still wondering about Emma Bovary's thought process in Flaubert's famous novel" or "What do I need to do for racism to disappear from the face of the earth?") and anything in between. We usually keep a friendly, upbeat tone, and we frequently post about projects we are working on. Since many of our clients are also our friends, we do not post "This project from client XYZ is killing me" if we are struggling with a project. You need to keep in mind that you are, first and foremost, a small-business owner. There are different theories on how much you should disclose about yourself to your friends and your clients, and there is no correct one. For instance, some entrepreneurs choose not to disclose their political views because they are worried they might not be hired for a specific job once their political views are public. Personally, we feel quite comfortable disclosing that information.

🐾 **Your info page.** This is the page where you can share whatever you would like about yourself with the Facebook community. There are standard fields that you can fill in, such as education, hobbies, jobs, favorite TV shows, etc. This is also the section that will list the Facebook groups you have joined. You can upload you profile picture, which will appear on your profile page. You can change it at any time, and make sure it is appropriate for both your personal and professional lives. Do not forget to link to your company website, your blog, or both.

Picture sharing. Facebook is a great place to create photo albums and share them with your friends. It is simpler than making an online album (think Picasa or Flickr) and sending the link to friends or family in a separate e-mail. However, Facebook limits the size of images, so it is not the best platform for high-resolution or artistic images. With Facebook, you can post your images, and all your contacts will see that you added them, can view them at their leisure, and even comment on them. We use this function not only for our personal images, but also to share pictures from conferences, presentations, and workshops. In terms of putting up pictures, we upload whatever we want to share with others, and ensure that we do not put up anything controversial. Whenever you put up a picture, ask yourself this question: are these pictures appropriate enough to share with clients and prospects? When in doubt, do not upload the image.

Others identifying you. While you can control which images you upload, you cannot control the actions of your friends and colleagues. Hopefully they will be smart enough not to upload images that could come back to haunt you later, but you never know. The way these images can be linked to you is by adding a tag with your name to the image, which is accomplished by clicking on the image and entering the person's name in the dialogue box. This image will then appear in both your own and your friend's photo section. If you would prefer the photo not be linked to you (Bad hair day in the 80s? Too much Long Island Iced Tea at graduation? Ex-boyfriend your husband does not care for?), you can simply remove the tag, and voilà. The image will be gone from your page, but not from your friend's. Now, if people recognize you behind all that 90s make-up and double scrunchies in your hair, we cannot help you.

Being smart and safe on Facebook

This might be redundant and obvious, but anything you put up can be seen by all your friends. In addition, when you write on someone's "wall" (which is the equivalent of a short message, visible to all), keep in mind that your comment will be visible to all friends. You should refrain from saying anything that is meant to be private. In addition, keep the crazy pictures of yourself to yourself.

Many times, fellow translators are worried about internet security, and while no system is infallible, Facebook is fairly safe, as only people who are your friends can see your information. You can make as little or as much information about yourself available as you would like, and Facebook will never ask you for sensitive data of any kind, such as a social security number.

http://mox.ingenierotraductor.com

© 2009 Alejandro Moreno-Ramos

CHAPTER 4

§▲

MARKETING

What is marketing?

According to the American Marketing Association, "Marketing is the activity, set of institutions, and processes for creating, communicating, delivering, and exchanging offerings that have value for customers, clients, partners, and society at large."[1] In order to build or expand your business, you need to market your services, find new customers, and turn your new customers into repeat customers.

New customers

New customers are the toughest ones to acquire, and they naturally require much more time and effort than repeat customers. The prevailing wisdom is that it is much easier, and much less expensive, to retain a current client than to allocate the resources needed to find a new client. It will be time-consuming to make contact with prospects and to turn them into new clients, so you always want to strive for repeat customers. Repeat customers are new customers first, so you will not be able to get around new client acquisition.

Do you have enough customers?

The truth is that you can never have enough customers. Even though you might be so well-situated at the moment that you cannot accept any new customers, you need to look toward the future and have a long-term plan. What if, for one reason or another, you lose some or all of these customers? It is not a good idea to

1   http://www.marketingpower.com/AboutAMA/Pages/DefinitionofMarketing.aspx

rely on your current customer base as your sole source of income for the future, as things can change. You need to market your services at all times. While you might not need to invest a lot of time and energy into new customer acquisition at any given time, you should always keep an eye open for new opportunities and new customers.

Repeat customers

Your long-term success will depend, in no small part, on your ability to do business with repeat customers. Many studies have found that it is a lot cheaper for the services provider – you – to keep a current client happy than it is to acquire a new one. Common sense tells you that, but what are you really doing to find and retain those repeat customers? How much time would you like to spend on acquiring this type of customer?

Build your relationships with customers. Just having an outstanding product or service is, unfortunately, not always enough to impress them.

&. It is a great idea to **follow up with a customer** within a few days of turning in a project to see if they have any additional questions or if there is anything else you can do. Your clients will be happy that you checked to see if there were any problems integrating your work into the final product. Offer your assistance. You might be surprised how unusual it is for most contractors to follow up on their work.

&. If you know your customer is under time pressure, you could **offer to deliver large projects in smaller batches**. Before you do this, check with your customer if this is something that would be beneficial for the workflow. Delivering in smaller batches might not be that convenient for you, because in latter parts of the project and upon final revision you might change some terminology. However, if it benefits your customer, you should do it.

&. **Check in with your favorite clients at the beginning of the month** to ask them about the status of their projects so you can reserve adequate time for them. This is not only a proactive way to handle your business, but it also potentially gives you more control over your project workflow.

&. **Go the extra mile.** Turn in a project early if you can. Volunteer to help your client find services you do not provide (other languages, specializations). Offer analysis and suggestions upon customer request. Be generous with your knowledge, even if you are not getting paid for it. Sometimes you have to give first.

Once you have built those relationships, your customers will be less sensitive to price and you will be able to reap the rewards. Customers want to receive good value for their money. Hopefully you will be such an integral part of their international strategy that your customer would not want to hire another vendor, even if it were less expensive to do so.

Pricing for repeat customers

Your ultimate goal is to turn new customers into repeat customers. In order to achieve this, you first and foremost need to deliver great service and a fantastic product. Then you need to make yourself memorable. Here are a few examples of how to turn a new customer into a repeat customer:

&. **Create a relevant pricing strategy** that will benefit both you and the client. For instance, when a client requests a website translation, ask whether the site will need continuous updates and changes to it after the original translation. If it does, consider giving the client a flat fee for all the updates after the initial translation. That way, your client can easily budget for it. Do not set the flat fee too low, because you might not know in the beginning how many updates will be coming your way. Consider adding a line to your price quote stating that you reserve the right to review this pricing strategy after the first month or some other reasonable time period. A flat fee is convenient for customers because they do not have to renegotiate with you every time, thus saving them time and money. An option is to charge a flat fee for your time, for instance, five hours' translation services. This way, a customer can send short bits of information and you simply keep track of the time it took you to translate them. This is an excellent way to add value for your customers by helping decrease their costs.

&. **While we generally do not recommend negotiating on the price per unit (or hour, or line)**, sometimes you may need to offer a customer a customized rate to incentivize her to become a repeat customer. Obtaining long-term repeat business is fantastic, because it will allow you to forecast your earnings more accurately. A few years ago, we entered into negotiations with a large company that had indicated the need for translations on a weekly basis. Many potential customers will simply say that there will be lots of business for you in the future, whether that is true or not. Some prospects might say this simply to obtain a lower price, so you have to take it with a grain of salt. In this case, the customer seemed genuinely interested in our services and we had a good feeling about the potential relationship. He kept on asking for a "repeat customer discount," which we did not offer and had not thought about offering. We went back and forth for a while, and then decided to grant him the minimal per-word discount that he was looking for. To this date, he is one of only two customers who receive this rate. He was true to his word, and he has been one of our best customers for many years. This strategy saved everyone time and headaches in the long run. After the initial negotiation, we never again talked about price and he never tried to haggle. We had agreed on a price, and no price quotes were ever necessary. We would simply send an invoice for the agreed-upon price after finishing each project. Payment was always prompt and reliable: truly a win-win situation.

&. **Make it stick out.** Include a handwritten note giving the customer a small one-time discount on the next translation and attach it to your printed invoice with a sticky note. It has the impact of a miniature ad. Customers will read the colorful note first; however, the message should be short and concise so it can be read in less than 10 seconds. And maybe they will stick it somewhere near the computer and thus see your "ad" all the time.

For more information on pricing strategies, please read the pricing chapter.

Are you losing customers?

In every business, it is part of the normal business cycle to lose some customers over time. Losing a customer does not mean you are not doing a good job, since it might be for reasons that are beyond your control. However, you can control a lot of things that might cause you to lose customers. If you feel that you are losing customers because they are dissatisfied, you need to take a hard look at your interaction with these customers and figure out how you can improve the relationship and perhaps retain them. The following are a few reasons for which you could lose a customer:

&. **Changes at your customer's company.** Many times, your relationship with a particular company will be based mainly on a single contact. If that contact leaves the company, especially if he/she holds an important position, it is quite possible that your relationship with the company might end. Sometimes, with a change in management, many or all existing vendors might be shown the door. It is might not fair, but it happens quite frequently.

&. **Customers going out of business.** Especially in tough economic times, many businesses have to close their doors. Account for the fact that some of your customers might not survive economic downturns. Plan accordingly and do not stop looking for new customers.

Customers no longer need your services. Customers' needs change: perhaps the company has decided to hire an in-house linguist or is no longer focusing on international business.

Customers are not happy with your services. This is a factor you can control. Whenever possible, you should have a conversation with your customers: why are they not happy? Is it because you cannot make unrealistic deadlines happen? In this case, you might be better off without that customer. Or is it because they perceive that they are not getting a good deal or good service? As difficult as it might be, try to have an honest, open conversation and avoid getting defensive. Can this relationship be salvaged? More importantly: do you want to salvage it? The Italian economist Wilfred Pareto got it right: according to the Pareto principle, 80% of your business will come from 20% of your customers.[2] Certain customers might not be good for your business. It sounds cruel, but as an entrepreneur, you have the liberty to choose who you work for. The term "firing customers" seems a bit too aggressive to us, but the idea behind it is good. If your customer is unreasonable, takes up too much of your time, does not pay on time, has unrealistic deadlines, or constantly haggles on price, it might be time to sever your relationship. If you feel that a good customer is leaving because you committed an error (or many), extend an honest apology and try to mend the relationship.

Customers choose another vendor. It is a competitive marketplace, and unless you have signed an exclusive contract with your customer, which is uncommon in our business, you do not have a repeat business guarantee. Your customers strive to optimize their operations and to find the vendors that best work for them. Some companies evaluate their vendors on a yearly basis and make changes as they see fit. Losing a customer that way is disappointing, but it is also part of the natural business cycle.

Build a brand

You will not be able to get repeat customers if they cannot remember your name or are unable to find you. You want to be the name that comes to mind when decision-makers are ready to hire a freelance translator or interpreter. Ideally, your name would be at the tip of these executives' tongues. You can achieve this by building a brand and by making continuous contact. Your to-do list:

---

2   http://management.about.com/cs/generalmanagement/a/Pareto081202.htm

ᕦ Get a logo. This does not have to be fancy or expensive – it could just be your initials. Have an Illustrator-savvy friend draw it or barter for the service with a graphic design student at your local community college. Our colleague, German/Swedish/Norwegian to English translator Tom Ellett bought his fantastic logo (http://www.albascan.com) from graphic designer Sandra Busta (http://www.poletopoleconsulting.com). Sandra is offering a logo discount to readers of this book. Another idea is to hold a so-called design contest for your logo. You can determine how much you would like to pay for your logo and then pick the design you like the best. We are a bit uneasy with this business model, because it is similar to translation sites that make translators compete on very low prices, so be fair and pay adequate prices for other professionals' services. Try http://99designs.com or http://www.astada.com/.

ᕦ Put the logo everywhere. It should be on your business cards, your letterhead, your quotes, your invoices, your address labels, your website, etc. Reinforcement and repetition are key.

ᕦ Continuous meaningful contact. This will be good for your relationship building, and it will also remind your customers who you are. In addition, they will see your nice logo on your letterhead and return address label. A quick thank-you note (e-mail is fine) saying that you have received payment is also a good idea, especially if the payment was processed quickly. If you can afford to spend roughly $15 a month, consider signing up with Constant Contact (http://www.constantcontact.com), the leader in e-mail marketing services for small businesses. They will help you create professional HTML e-mails, and you will not need any tech skills. It would be even less expensive if you found an HTML-savvy friend to help you create just one or two HTML e-mails that you could send throughout the year.

Become a customer concierge

One of the easiest ways to become a customer concierge is to take notes. First of all, pay attention when your customer is talking to you, either in person or over the phone, and take as many notes as you can while fully focusing on what the customer is saying. Consider repeating to your customer what she has just said, for instance: "To recap, you would like your brochure translated from French into Tagalog by next Sunday..." This will make it apparent to the customer that you have been paying attention and that you understand what she wants. You could also send a quick recap as a follow-up e-mail after the conversation if you would prefer to have it all in writing. Take a few minutes after the conversation ends to quickly type up everything you have discussed with your client. You might think you will remember all the details, but if you have enough customers, you will not. If your customer happens to mention that she will not be available for a few weeks because she is having surgery, consider sending flowers (if and when appropriate). If your customer mentions that her accounting department is difficult to deal with, ask her how you can make the process easier and write down what she says; then follow the instructions. Has your client repeatedly mentioned that getting the documents ready for you to translate is a time-consuming and not very efficient process? Perhaps you can offer your project management skills or volunteer to start on the first part of the project while the rest is still being compiled. Does your customer dislike Microsoft Office? Consider e-mailing the final documents in Open Office (www.openoffice.org) – it is free and it will take you only a few seconds to save in that format. Is your client a night owl or a morning person? Does your client have a BlackBerry that also functions has her main office phone number? That is good to know so you do not call late at night just to leave a non-urgent message on what you believe to be an unattended office phone. Does your customer like faxing documents? Do you see yourself running to your local copy shop every time she wants something faxed? If this is one of your main customers, consider getting a fax machine or online fax service. It is the cost of doing business, even if you think the technology is quite outdated (which it is). Strive to make the transaction easy on the customer. For an easy way to compare online fax services, try http://www.faxcompare.com.

Competitive advantage

Competitive advantage is a widely-used business term. According to Michael Porter, "A competitive advantage exists when the firm is able to (…) deliver benefits that exceed those of competing products (differentiation advantage). Thus, a competitive advantage enables the firm to create superior value for its customers and superior profits for itself."[3] Basically, a competitive advantage is what you or your company is better at than your competitors; it is what sets you apart from your competition.

Find your competitive advantage

What are you really good at (beyond the obvious translation and/or interpretation skills)? What are you better at than your colleagues?

Many translator postings on large translation websites say "fast, reliable, high quality." These really are not selling points, but merely the bare minimum of what every purchaser of language services should get. Unfortunately, while customers rightly expect these services to be of top-notch quality, that is not always the case. However, that still does not mean that you should compete solely on the basics. If your potential customer sees twenty postings with these three adjectives, how would they choose? You guessed it: probably randomly. Provide some

3   http://www.quickmba.com/strategy/competitive-advantage/

more information about what it is that you are exceptionally good at, about what sets you apart from your competition. This is your competitive advantage.

Examples of competitive advantages

A few examples of competitive advantages include: 24-hour service, working as a translation and editing team, offering conference interpretation services on holidays, etc. During the many workshops we have given around the U.S. and Europe, we group linguists in groups of two or three to interview each other and find out what their competitive advantage is. After this 10-minute brainstorming session, those who would like to share the results with the group briefly discuss their findings. Most of the time, linguists already have a good idea of what their competitive advantage is – they just have not used it to market themselves. During those sessions, we have heard from folks with the following outstanding competitive advantages:

&. **Holding a Ph.D. in the field.** One attendee had a Ph.D. in a very specific technical field, which is his main translation specialization. This has served him very well, and as far as he knows, he is the only translator holding a Ph.D. in this field. He uses his strong academic credentials in conjunction with his solid translation experience as a selling point on all his marketing materials.

&. **Being fully bicultural.** While many interpreters learn their source language later in life, others are privileged to have grown up with two or more languages, usually the result of parents' careers (diplomacy, international corporations with headquarters in foreign countries) or living in a bilingual household. In addition to bilingualism, biculturalism is a big plus for an interpreter. By fully knowing and understanding both the source and the target language's culture, the interpreter has the ability to comprehend all the nuances and undertones of the language. This is a significant competitive advantage, and one of our workshop's attendees always includes "fully bicultural and bilingual in Spanish and English" in her marketing materials.

&. **Having in-depth knowledge of your specialization.** We heard from a participant who had worked in international finance for many years before making the switch to full-time financial translation. "15 years' experience at top-notch financial institutions" or "Financial translator and 10 years' working experience as a financial analyst for Deutsche Bank" would be good ways to advertise her services. This would clearly communicate that she understands the subject area very well. Having an insider's understanding of the inner workings of the financial world sets this translator apart and constitutes her competitive advantage.

{&. **Holding a government clearance certification.** If you work with a lot of government contractors or directly with government agencies, holding a security clearance or any other type of relevant government-related certification can be of great benefit to you.

{&. **Delivering results.** This is similar to the "good, reliable, fast" descriptions that you should stay away from, but with a different twist. As mentioned before, customers expect great service, on-time delivery, and a professional transaction, as they should. Unfortunately, not all linguists deliver that, and customers have mentioned to us in the past that only a few interpreters responded to a request for proposal. Hence, it is evident that not all linguists meet clients' expectations of quality, professionalism, and responsiveness, which is true for any industry. As a result, if you truly excel at delivering world-class service, say so. Just phrase it a bit differently so your competitive advantage does not look like everyone else's.

Competitive advantage brainstorming

Go beyond the overused adjectives and find out what sets you apart from your competition. It does not have to be simple a list of adjectives; it could also be a short, easy-to-remember phrase. Talk to a loved one, a colleague or even a client. It might take you some time to clearly determine what your competitive advantage is, so do not rush. Once you identify the competitive advantage, try to determine approximately how many other professionals share it. While no competitive advantage is truly unique, it is best to have a competitive advantage that is shared by as few colleagues as possible. Once you have settled on your competitive advantage, use it as the basis of your marketing strategy.

Cold calling/e-mailing

Cold calling has a very low success rate and is not the most promising approach nor the best use of your time. According to Joanne Black, cold calling has a success rate of 2%.[4] If you have a long list of non-qualified leads on hand and have the ability to quickly create personalized letters through mail merge or e-mails and you do not have another, more pressing or potentially more lucrative project

---

4   Joanne Black. *No More Cold Calling™: The Breakthrough System That Will Leave Your Competition in the Dust* (New York: Business Plus, 2007).

lined up, our advice is to go ahead and do it. It is a lot of work, and you need to learn to deal with negative responses or a complete lack thereof. In general, your time is better spent on more targeted efforts. For example, approaching parties who have already expressed interest in your service (i.e., subscribers to your e-newsletter) is a better approach that tends to be more successful, both in the short and long term. Please be aware that in German-speaking countries, restrictions on cold calling have been introduced. In Austria, the Telecommunications Acts prohibits businesses from calling other businesses offering their services without obtaining the other businesses' consent ahead of time. The same is true for e-mails, text messages, and faxes, but does not apply to marketing materials sent in the mail. However, since the strict application and execution of this law would basically bring a lot of businesses' marketing activities to a halt, people still accept cold calls. In Germany and Switzerland, similar laws have been introduced. However, "traditional phone marketing" is allowed in Switzerland, while automated phone calls are prohibited unless prior consent to these phone calls has been given. Check your local legislation before getting started. Even if cold calling is permissible by law, we do not recommend using it as your main strategy, but merely as a backup plan. Getting introduced to prospects through a common connection is a much better approach.

The art of getting an introduction

Growing up in Mexico, we were quite intrigued by a seemingly archaic ritual. For example, let us say you are a young man at a club or bar having a fun evening out with your friends. We will call you Francisco. Then you see a girl who catches your eye. We will call her Alejandra, whom Francisco does not know yet. What to do next? Protocol and etiquette would prevent Francisco from doing what he do in the U.S. – going up to the girl and introducing himself. Thus, he would spend most of the evening roaming the venue in the hopes of finding someone who knows Alejandra so he or she can make the proper introduction. Sounds cumbersome, right? However, the person making the introduction – who knows both parties – would vouch for both Francisco and Alejandra. The contact is therefore instantly elevated to a new level of confidence, and people tend to feel more relaxed. In Mexico, this is called "*presentar*" (literally, to introduce). For our purposes, we will call it the art of non-cold calling. How can you apply this lesson to your practice?

   Identify a person you would like to pitch to.

   Search your networks (online and offline) for someone who knows both of you.

🍂 **Formally ask for an introduction.** Do not make any assumptions. Just because both of you know a third person does not mean that your contact is going to be willing to make the introduction. Your contact will be vouching for you with his or her connection, so you need to view this introduction as an honor, not a right. The best way to do this is to formally state, either in person or in writing, your goal of meeting the specified person, and to clearly outline what you would like to get out of this introduction. Be honest and straightforward and do not hide your intention of doing business. Wanting to meet someone to tell him or her about your services is perfectly acceptable in the business world.

🍂 **Offer to take both parties to lunch.** In some cases, the person making the introduction might suggest an informal meeting between all three of you. If this is going to take place outside the office, you need to be sure to pick up the restaurant tab. In order to make it very clear who is paying, you can either give your credit card to the waiter during a discreet trip to the restroom or say "I will take the check" as you are getting ready to ask for the bill. Also, clearly communicate your intentions to the folks you plan on taking out: "I would be honored if you would accept my invitation to an informal business lunch to discuss my ideas" is a good way to phrase it.

🍂 **Copy the person who introduced you on your first e-mail to new contact.** If your contact with your desired new connection begins in the virtual world, be sure to copy the "matchmaker" on the first e-mail communication you have with your new potential client. The person who made the introduction most likely would enjoy being in the loop on the development of this new professional contact, and by copying them, you will save yourself another e-mail to the introducer reporting on the status of the meeting. Copying them on subsequent e-mails is probably not necessary – but when in doubt, ask.

🍂 **Regardless of the outcome, send a thank-you note (e-mail is fine) to the person who made the connection.** Whether this introduction leads to any business for you or not is not that relevant. What is important is that you properly acknowledge the introducer's time and effort.

Specialization and non-specialization

In translation circles, there is a lot of discussion about specialization. While this is an essential issue, most of us usually have a pretty good idea of our specializations. However, do you know which area(s) you do not specialize in?

🍃 **Non-specialization.** Find what yours is (or are) and stick to them. Do not accept projects in these specific areas. For us, one area is in-depth medical translations. Beyond doing patient-focused health care translations, we stay away from higher-level medical texts, such as oncology reports. If we get an inquiry about these types of translations, we gladly refer the business to colleagues who specialize in medical translations.

🍃 **Ethical obligation.** We all have an ethical and a professional obligation to only accept projects that we are qualified to translate or interpret. Sometimes, those will be areas that are closely related to our specializations. In general, you are setting yourself up for failure by accepting a project with which you just do not feel comfortable. Do not give in to client pressure urging you to accept a project. Ultimately, if there are problems with the end product, this will reflect negatively on you, regardless of how much you insisted that this was not your area of expertise. Doing a favor for a client could quickly jeopardize the reputation you have built for yourself. This is the time to recommend a colleague with substantially more experience in the field in question.

🍃 **The Warren Buffett approach.** This well-respected billionaire investor's advice on buying stocks is really good: choose stocks and companies to invest in based on whether you understand their product or service. Warren Buffett famously said: "Investment must be rational; if you do not understand it, do not do it."[5] The idea can be applied to specializations: choose one or more based on your interests, passions, previous knowledge, and whether or not you understand the field.

🍃 **Organic development.** Sometimes, a specialization can develop organically and over time, including when a repeat customer expands into a related business field. That is a natural progression and should be a smooth transition. In our case, we have done this with several customers, and have added several fields of specialization (some of them quite narrow, such as water resources management in the American West) along the way. Do not be afraid to branch out into related fields and areas: the beginning might be research-intensive, but if you feel like you have a solid base from a related field, this is a fantastic way to increase your areas of knowledge and specialization.

---

5   Mary Buffett and David Clark, *The Tao of Warren Buffett: Warren Buffett's Words of Wisdom: Quotations and Interpretations to Help Guide You to Billionaire Wealth and Enlightened Business Management* (New York: Scribner), 2006.

Do this, but not that

🍂 **Do not** try to market or sell to people who have told you that they have no interest in or need for your services.

🍂 **Do not** purposely try to pitch to a client who you know is already in good hands with a colleague – it is a free market, but still, you need to be fair.

🍂 **Do** follow up with potential clients who explicitly state that they are not interested at the moment, but that they would like to hear from you again at a specific point in the future.

🍂 **Do** try to read between the lines. Some potential customers might not be straightforward enough to tell you "no." Learn how to interpret the signals and do not approach them if you have the feeling that they are not interested.

Relationship building

Any businessperson needs to look at the time they invest in new and current customers as long-term investments. Just like in personal relationships, building professional relationships takes time and effort. You never know if a prospect who is not interested in your services right now could become a customer in the future – say, if their company's mindset changes, if they leave for a different company that is in need of language services, or if they want to recommend you to a friend. It is always very important to treat every person you come in contact with as a potential customer (or friend of a potential customer). Just like in personal relationships, this does not mean that you should always agree to everything that is being proposed to you. Simply act like the professional that you are, negotiate in good faith when needed, and agree to terms and conditions that you feel comfortable with. You will most likely need to make contact with potential clients several times before any business comes your way, so do not be discouraged if you do not get a project right away. Be sure not to cross the fine line between following up with potential leads and becoming annoying by sending too many unsolicited e-mails or making too many unsolicited phone calls. There is no hard rule for this, and many potential providers, in any industry, can be quite aggressive about the way they pursue business. It is a good idea to let the customer know that you are available without being pushy or calling too often. That said, there are a few things that you should keep in mind if you want your relationship with customers to be solid and mutually beneficial:

‌ Listen to what the prospect is saying. If you are told that their language services needs will be re-evaluated next quarter, ask if it is acceptable that you contact them again at that point in time. If the prospect mentions that they would like to hear from you by the end of the month, make a note to do so and follow up. If a person is telling you that she does not have a need for your services at the moment, and that she does not expect this to change, but will contact you if it does, respect that and refrain from following-up again. Do not sound desperate, and make sure that your customer knows that you are listening to them and that you are honoring their requests.

‌ Do not add anyone to your distribution list without their explicit permission. Surely this has happened to you before: you have a correspondence exchange with someone, and next thing you know, you are on their newsletter distribution list without having requested it. Before you add anyone to your distribution list, ask for their permission.

‌ Send holiday cards. Regardless of whether you have done business with the person in question or not, it is always appropriate to send a holiday card – but just be sure you do not incorrectly thank the client for the past year's business if there has not been any. Keep good records on your prospects and current customers. For potential customers, a brief holiday greeting and "Looking forward to working with you in the future" is appropriate.

‌ Send small gifts if you can. While no one will expect a small business to send lavish gifts, consider making small gifts to your most important customers on special occasions, such as holidays or company anniversaries. Most companies already receive a wealth of practical, but unoriginal items such as notepads, pens, mouse pads, etc. In order to set yourself apart from the rest, put some thought into coming up with something creative and clever. You do not want to be just another vendor who sends an overpriced and quickly forgotten fruit and cheese basket. Consider sending locally made specialty products or a highly customized gift that you know the person will enjoy. We recently received a very handy USB stick embedded in a traditional wooden Dutch shoe, which was hand painted and simply gorgeous. It was the creative gift of Dutch translators Annie Tadema and Astrid van der Weert (www.tw-vertalingen.com). While these fantastic gifts are quite expensive (EUR 12 each if you order 50; cost decreases with higher quantities), they make a lasting impression.

As difficult as it may seem, try not to take it personally when someone tells you they do not need your services or are not going to work with you. Many times, this simply means that they do not have adequate resources available or they do not have a need for language services. No one is saying that you are not a good linguist, but that you might just not be in the right place at the right time. Take a deep breath, thank your contact person for their time, make a note of when you last spoke to the person or archive the e-mail, think long-term, and move on. Developing thick skin is essential in the business world.

Get some media coverage

A low-cost, but labor intensive way of getting your name known is trying to get some media coverage. Even though print journalism is facing significant long-term challenges, most towns still have one or several newspapers, and many large cities will have neighborhood papers. Spend some time pitching to local editors in the hopes of getting profiled. If they are not interested, ask if they would be willing to print your press release. Keep the following in mind:

Make it easy on the editor. Do not call or e-mail a newspaper or magazine that does not regularly feature small-business owners. Do some research before you approach the editor. Decrease the editor's workload by preparing a specific angle that they could take on the subject. While they might go in a different direction or not be interested at all, it shows that you are serious and prepared.

Provide background information. If an editor appears interested, e-mail as much relevant information about yourself as you can.

Establish common ground If you are a regular reader of the publication, say so. Mention a previous article that you read in the publication that you really enjoyed.

Do not be discouraged. Journalists are traditionally under tremendous time constraints, especially editors. Just because they choose not to write about you does not mean you do not have an interesting story. It might just not fit their editorial direction or be in an area that they already cover frequently. Also, remember that print journalists must bring newsworthy and interesting articles to their readers, and you can be sure that you are not the only small-business owner who approaches the media. There is traditionally only a small amount of space reserved for business profiles, so keep that in mind.

๛ Try again. Last year, Judy approached a local community newspaper, which does weekly business profiles, about getting featured in their publication. The reporter was very interested, but the editor was not. While that was certainly a bit disheartening, Judy was lucky enough to get mentioned in a Wall Street Journal article later that year.[6] Armed with that article, Judy approached the community newspaper again.

Online press releases

Publishing online press releases is a good strategy to try to increase your online footprint and your exposure. As opposed to the services offered by major press agencies such as the Associated Press, these services are free. The downside is that your press release will probably not get picked up by any high-profile media, but the main point is online exposure for you. Many print journalists keep an eye on these free online release services and it is quite possible that some smaller publications will hear about you, especially those in your same geographic area. Most online press release sites index quite high in search engines, meaning that if someone types your name, the press releases will come up toward the top of the search results. Register with one or two free press release services and submit a few articles. It should not take you more than thirty minutes, and it will get relevant information about you onto the internet. Most of the free services will not include hyperlinks to your site unless you upgrade to premium, which we do not necessarily recommend. However, the link to your site will still appear; it just will not be clickable. If you have a memorable business name, hopefully users will just open a new window in their browser and search for your business. When writing press releases, keep the following in mind:

๛ **Be relevant.** Many things simply are not newsworthy, and you should stay away from them, because if you do not, you might alienate people who are genuinely interested in your services. An example of irrelevant information would be: "The Spanish Wizard Bought a New Mac Today." However, writing "The Spanish Wizard Announces Companywide Implementation of New American Ethics Standards in Translation" is much more relevant. Can you see the difference? Think of yourself as a customer or as a reader. What would you like to know? Not all of your info has to be sales-oriented. It is a perfectly good idea to send out a press release about having been elected to an office at your state or local translation and interpretation association, announcing the acquisition of a new client (with the client's permission, of course), etc.

---

6   http://online.wsj.com/article/SB10001424052748703558004574582012163556106.html

Be brief. Your press release should be no longer than three to six paragraphs, excluding the final paragraph that starts with "About (your company)". Ideally, when seen on a website, users should not have to scroll past the fold of the page (i.e. they would see all the information without having to scroll).

Come up with a good headline. The art of press release writing has been intensely studied by every public relations major and been perfected by agencies across the globe. It is not easy to catch the reader's attention, and there is a fine line between having a headline that is much too long and one that does not have enough information. When in doubt, keep it short.

Do not send out too many press releases. We receive dozens of press releases a week, and sometimes we receive up to five a week from the same company, which has the unfortunate effect of diluting that company's brand because they think that everything is newsworthy – it is not. Choose wisely: a press release every few months should really be sufficient.

Get creative. Many times, linguists do not know what to write about their businesses. Once you sit down to think about it, you will realize that there is indeed a lot to say. Again, put yourself in the customers' shoes. Whatever you write on the press release is information that your customers will very easily find about you. You are in the lucky position to be able to control that information. Did you just launch a new website? Did you just pass your translation certification exam? Have you been selected as the guest speaker at a conference? Consider writing a press release about it.

Choose good press release distribution services. We like the clean interface of www.free-press-release.com. The downside of this free service is that the system will constantly ask you to upgrade to the fee-based premier version. If you make a typo or see an error after the release is live, you will not be able to fix it online unless – you guessed it – you upgrade to the premier version. Or recommendation is to write the releases in your favorite word processing program and then copy and paste from there. We also think that www.openpr.com is a great site. It is based in Germany, but will distribute your information in the U.S. (you can also choose the German site). The interface is in English, and these releases are reviewed by editors, so your release will not be live for a day or so. There are very strict editorial guidelines, as they are looking for news, not sales pitches, and their team frequently reject releases that do not meet the editorial guidelines. This is a great site to learn about press release writing, as the guidelines are thorough and well thought-out.

How much time should you be spending on this? Spend 30 minutes on this every few months or so, more often if you have something interesting and newsworthy to communicate. Start a press release folder on your directory structure and save every release as well as a template, so you can just copy and paste the "About Us" information every time, thus saving time and effort.

Press release sample

Our small business, Twin Translations, issued the following release in the fall of 2008. We decided to share it with you so you can see an example of a press release that we think is quite effective.

For Immediate Release   Contact: Judy Jenner, (702) 541-4647

Las Vegas-Based Twin Translations Goes Green

Las Vegas, Nev. (November 18, 2008) Twin Translations, a boutique translation and copywriting business owned by two seasoned linguists, announces its efforts to move toward a paperless office.

The company's owners, Judy and Dagmar Jenner, were born in Austria, where eco-friendly initiatives have existed for decades, and grew up in Mexico City, where protecting the planet has traditionally not been a priority. Judy Jenner in Las Vegas and Dagmar Jenner, who lives and works in Vienna, Austria, want to do their part in ensuring our planet will be healthy and clean for future generations.

Even though the company has always operated under the green principle, Twin Translations is now kicking it up a notch. The company contacted all its banking partners in the U.S. and Europe and signed up for paperless banking, which includes not receiving cancelled paper checks. In addition, all invoicing to customers is done electronically, thus not generating any unnecessary paper waste. All new dictionaries to be purchased will be purchased in digital format.

Twin Translation's environmental commitment goes beyond cutting back on paper: Judy Jenner has driven a Prius for several years, thus reducing her carbon footprint. Dagmar Jenner has chosen to completely forego a car in Vienna and relies on public transportation and walking. Since both partners operate their businesses out of their homes, there is no commute to work and no polluting.

About Twin Translations:

Twin Translations specializes in legal, business, marketing, travel and tourism, and e-commerce translations in English<->Spanish, English<->German and Spanish<->German. In addition, Twin Translations does extensive copywriting in three languages for clients around the world.

Twin Translations' owners are Judy and Dagmar Jenner, identical twins who were born in Austria and grew up in a trilingual household in Mexico City. With multiple college and graduate degrees from institutions on both continents between them, and work experience in four countries, Twin Translations' owners have the language knowledge, educational background, and real-life work experience to convey their clients' messages accurately and effectively.

Marketing materials

High-quality marketing materials will be one of the best investments you will make in your business. When we say marketing materials, we certainly do not mean résumés. Remember that this book focuses on working with direct customers, and trust us: your potential customers do not want to see your résumé. They are neither hiring you for a permanent position nor are they familiar with the latest version of whatever translation memory tool you might be using. This information is of no relevance to them.

The case against résumés

Do you think other vendors, such as software companies, office furniture supplier, or interior decorators send out the résumés of the company's owners to potential customers? They typically do not do that, and neither should you. You need to spend the time and effort to develop marketing materials. When we first started doing this, years ago, it was not unusual for our marketing materials to be the only non-résumés at an entire translation and interpretation conference. It could be considered a new approach, but is really just a natural extension of the way we run our business. Back to basics: think of yourself as a customer. If you were a customer, what information would you like to have about your potential vendor? No one will read a two-page résumé. When pitching to direct clients, you will most likely be contacting folks who are very busy, such as directors of marketing, heads of the communications department, or high-ranking executives in the marketing department. Make it easy for them to make a purchasing decision. It should not be up to them to filter through your detailed résumé to try to determine whether you would be a good vendor. That is your job. You need to create customized materials for most companies you approach. You can easily do this by creating several basic templates and changing a few sentences as needed.

Here are a few things you should communicate in your marketing materials:
1. What you can do for the company.
2. Your relevant experience, targeted for the company you are approaching.

3. Why they should entrust you with their language services.
4. Basic information about your academic background.
5. Details about your competitive advantage.

Developing good marketing materials

While there are really no limits to how creative you can get with your materials in terms of design, layout, or content, there are a few elements that all marketing materials should have. It does not matter whether your presentation is a tri-fold brochure, a one-page document, or a glossy postcard-sized flyer: it should be well thought-out, precise, and targeted.

≈ **Professional photo.** While vacation pictures are priceless memories, this is not the place to use them. Your professional marketing materials should include a professional photo. Try to find someone with a good camera to take a few nice pictures of you. At the very least, ask a friend or partner to take a well-lit headshot of you against a neutral background. Professional portraits are your best option, but unfortunately they can be too expensive for small businesses. That is why we think bartering is a great idea – there is a reason bartering has been around for thousands of years. In our case, we take new pictures once a year, and our friend and photographer Ulf Buchholz does them for us. He has a very high-end camera and a good eye for what works well on film. We usually choose a few different locations, keeping in mind the customers we want to target. To create truly relevant images, we try to include our customers' businesses into our backgrounds, such as neon signs for images that we use for marketing materials designed for gaming companies. Ulf's services would be quite expensive, but our barter system includes taking Ulf to lunch, putting his copyright sign and name on all our images, and letting him use our pool all summer long. He lives in Las Vegas, and he does not have a pool; we do – so it is a mutually beneficial barter agreement. When taking pictures, consider taking different ones for different clients in an effort to make them as customized as possible. Examples:

≈ **Conservative images** (with business suit) for banking, financial, and customers in the legal profession.

≈ **More creative images** (with interesting clothes that show off your personality) for customers in the creative fields such as PR agencies, marketing companies, and travel and tourism-related businesses.

❧ Pictures of you in specialization-specific surroundings, such as in a lab if you work in pharmaceuticals and chemistry. If you specialize in literature, an image of you surrounded by books would work very well. If you translate in the automotive industry, why not take a picture centered around auto parts?

❧ High quality-paper. This is not the place to save money. Invest in nice, thick paper, especially if you will be handing these documents directly to senior executives. Choose a color other than white. Get creative: have postcards made. Your materials do not have to be restricted to letter-sized documents. Visit www.vistaprint.com for low-cost, professional-looking marketing materials.

❧ Update your materials. A few times a year, take a look at your marketing materials. Has anything changed? Have you joined a new professional organization or have you been elected to a board position? Add new customers and projects on a regular basis to ensure your materials include your latest and most relevant information. Keep the content fresh and updated.

❧ PDF everything. Every document that you send out via e-mail should be a PDF. This way, it will not only look much more professional, but it will also prevent others from editing your document. In addition, the layout and fonts will be retained independently of the recipient's software. It only takes a few seconds to turn any document into a PDF. If you do not want to spend money on the fee-based Adobe Acrobat PDF maker, consider this free open-source software PDF maker: www.pdfforge.org/products/pdf-creator.

No free business cards

As small-business owners, we need to look for places to decrease our expenses. However, there are areas in which we should not skimp. We call those the outward-facing categories. Your local copy shop usually has affordable business card services that are professional-looking and are ready within a week or so. As much as we like Vistaprint's services, do not use their free business card option. The catch with the free business card option is that Vistaprint uses those cards to promote their own business, which seems fair. This means that on the back of the business cards it will have a statement to the effect of "get your own free business cards at Vistaprint," so they are not a good option for a professional business. As soon as you upload your own logo and choose the paid option, this statement about free cards will not appear on the back of your business cards. The cost for these cards is still very reasonable. Keep an eye out for special savings events, when the cost is even lower than usual.

Get a website

In the summer of 2009, Judy wrote an article about websites for linguists for the July-August 2009 issue of the Institute of Translation and Interpreting's *Bulletin*. Since it is a useful summary of how linguists can get their own websites, we have taken some portions of the article and included it in this section. The article has been converted to American English, shortened, condensed to avoid redundancies with other chapters, adapted to fit the format of this book, and has been published with permission by the editor, Rachel Malcolm.

The $10 website

As language professionals in the 21st century, most of our professional lives happen online, and it is more paramount than ever that we have an online presence. There is no doubt that not having a solid website can result in less business. You certainly cannot measure the negative, that is, you simply do not know how many people are not contacting you because they cannot find you online, but rest assured that the number is probably quite significant.

Until now, having a professional website created and maintained had been a daunting task. As small-business owners, we all have to be money-savvy and certainly do not want to invest critical funds into what can be perceived as a non-critical activity (which in reality it is not). Throughout the years, colleagues have cited many reasons for their lack of a web presence, including lack of HTML skills, limited budget, being too busy, or not knowing a good web designer.

Now, thanks to our friends at Google, we are running out of excuses as to why we do not have a website. There is no more need to find a web guru, no more meetings with the designer trying to figure out what you want and how much this will cost, and no more exorbitant hosting fees. You have heard correctly: this is cheap, quick, and good, which sounds almost too good to be true. It is not – read on.

A note before we get started: there is a lot to say in favor of professional web designers. They are usually fantastic web professionals with a vast amount of experience and the expertise to help you develop a solid web presence. As small-business owners, we also like to support other small professional services organizations, and if you can afford to spend a few hundred dollars, euros, or pounds, you might want to consider hiring a professional IT expert. However, if you are on a limited budget, you can create a website yourself, host it, register the URL, publish it, maintain it and update it; all for $10 a year. No special skills are required – if you can maintain your LinkedIn, Facebook, or Twitter page, you can build your own website. You will not have to touch the HTML code if you do not want to.

- **Get started.** Watch the user-friendly video tutorial, courtesy of Google: http://www.youtube.com/watch?v=fD-4FRTzxkI.

- **Join the Google family.** In order to use any of the free Google services, you will need a Google account, which is also free. If you already have an existing Gmail account, you can log in using that information. If you do not have one, go here: https://www.google.com/accounts/.

- **Get Google Apps:** This is a suite of applications that is also free of charge, and it includes Google Sites, which lets you create your own website. The Google Apps Standard edition, which you will be using, is free, but the domain name is $10 a year (get out your wallet). The user-friendly interface will let you check if your desired domain name is available. http://www.google.com/apps/intl/en/group/index.html. If the URL you want is not available, Google will suggest alternatives. This is a quick three-step process, after which you will be ready to start building your page. Google also has a handy blog dedicated exclusively to Google Sites and its applications. It contains helpful tips about how to best get the tools to work for you. http://googlesitesblog.blogspot.com/.

- **Choose your URL.** You need to put some serious thought into choosing your URL. The best way to do this is to hold a brainstorming session, either just you or you and a friend/business partner/significant other who knows your business well. What kind of message do you want to be sending to your customers? How can you be memorable? Have you already registered and incorporated a business? If yes, then you should use that URL, unless you want to re-name and re-brand your company. Try to come up with a non-generic URL that people can remember. For instance, www.spanishtranslator.com is too generic. On the other hand, www.spanishwizards.com or www.portugueseworld.com might be better options. Think of yourself as a customer: if you were looking for translation services, what kind of URLs would appeal to you? You should convey that you are competent, creative, and professional. Also, make sure that your URL is not too long. Remember that this is what you will be putting on your business cards, and on your marketing materials. Hence, www.spanishtranslationwizardsfromspain.com is too long. You would not be able to fit it on a regular-sized business card. Think short and sweet.

❧ **Choose your e-mail address.** Keep it simple. E-mail addresses such as home@xyz.com and office@xyz.com are good choices. In addition, any combination of your name is fine, too, either first name, last name, or both.

❧ **Write the content of the site.** Before you get into creating the actual site, you should decide how many sections you want to have and write the copy for them. While you can certainly do this while you are creating the actual pages, it makes the process speedier and more streamlined if you know which sections you will have. For most translators, having sections such as About, Contact, Background, Services, Rates, Clients, Testimonials, Blog, etc. are good ideas. Write whichever sections you want to start out with. You can keep on building upon what you have already created at any point in the future.

❧ **Choose the colors, theme, and layout.** Google Sites is template-based, which means that all you have to do is plug content into pre-defined templates, analogous to Facebook and LinkedIn. You will not have a top-of-the-line website, but it will be nice and clean, with an easy navigation and layout. In terms of color and font: keep it simple. Dark font on a light background makes for easiest readability. Google offers a variety of backgrounds, and you can always change and update it (you can find this option under more actions/manage sites/colors and fonts as well as themes).

❧ **It is live!** Your pages (and any changes and updates) will be live immediately after you hit the "save" button. However, remember that the internet is a very big place, so do not worry about people finding your site when it is not quite ready. The reality is that you can almost be completely certain that no one will find your site unless you direct them to it. Take your time to fully create your site before you announce it. Allow yourself a few days (or weeks) to build the content and play around with the colors and backgrounds. The most important thing to remember is that nothing you do on your site is irreversible. If you find a typo, fix it.

❧ **Spread the word.** Now the real work begins. Having a website is a fantastic start, but it can only lead to business if potential customers can find it. Send out an e-mail announcing your website to all your friends, colleagues, and clients. Look through your LinkedIn contacts, your Rolodex and your address books, both virtual and paper, and send out a quick e-mail about your new venture. This is your first step in making it known that you have a website: telling everyone you know and asking them to tell their contacts, hence building word-of-mouth.

❧ Add new and fresh content to it. In general, a website indexes higher in search results and folks are more interested in it if it regularly features new content. There are several sections to which you can potentially add new items on a regular basis. The clients section would be a good option.

In addition, you could create a section with "speaking engagements" where you post any presentations that you have given or a section on "professional development" where you list the conferences you have attended or the ones at which you have presented.

By following these straightforward steps, you should be well on your way to creating a good-looking business website, all without spending more than $10 and a few hours of your time. Think of your web presence this way: if you only get one client all year and a $100 project, you will already have recouped your very small investment. No more excuses: do it. Close the book, turn on your computer, and get started.[7]

The art of online marketing

While this book will not provide a thorough online marketing guide – that is an entire book by itself, and we will leave that to the online marketing and search engine optimization gurus – we will give you some basics as well as hints and tips on how to avoid wasting your time online. At its most basic, the goal of online marketing is to sell your services online, mainly by driving traffic to your website or other online presence, from where people will hopefully get in touch with you.

Basic search engine optimization (SEO) for linguists

If you already have a professional website, you have laid the groundwork for search engine optimization. If you do not yet have a website, creating one should be on your to-do list. Unfortunately, just because you have a website does not mean that potential clients will find you. The internet, or the Wild Wild West, is a very big space. The challenge is making sure that people who do not know you or your URL, such as Jane Doe who is looking for "French translators in San Sebastián," find your website. How do you do that? Here are the basics of what you should know about search engine optimization (SEO) and search engine marketing (SEM).

---

7   Judy Jenner, "The £6 website in 12 easy steps," ITI Bulletin (July – August 2009): 20. Reprinted with permission of the ITI Bulletin.

No one really has the answers, except maybe the people at Google, Yahoo and MSN, and they are not telling. Many large e-commerce companies spend exorbitant amounts of money on search engine marketing consultants. Sure, they are quite good at what they do, but major search engines do not really like search marketers. Search engines constantly try to improve their algorithms to enhance user experience and provide good results to the users, not necessarily to advertising companies. This means that some days your site might come up on the first page of results, sometimes on the third, because sometimes variable X has more weight than Y in the search algorithms. Search engines do not publish their variables and their weight, so no one really knows how it all works. If you know, please share. If someone tells you that for a minimal fee they can guarantee you a top 10 ranking, do not believe them. However, for thousands of dollars, it is possible to get your page to the top of the rankings (via either pay-per-click or by buying links to high-profile pages, which are both prohibitively expensive for small businesses) in the short term.

If you do not want to spend money, you will have to put in the work. There are two ways to achieve a high ranking: via paid search and organic search. Paid search is the ads that the customer sees on the right-hand side of the search results, which are easily identifiable as ads. This is an option if you have some extra money to spend. However, research has shown that customers are frequently weary of ads and like to look at the organic results, which are all the results in the center of the page. For paid search, the specific price you will have to pay for a keyword depends on an auction. Keywords that generate very high traffic (think 'hotels', 'airline tickets', or in our case, 'translation', 'localization', etc.) are very expensive because large multinational corporations buy them. Keywords in niche markets are much less expensive (think 'Japanese legal translator in San Luis Obispo'). Most of us are better off trying to rank high on the organic searches. How do you do that? By having relevant, frequently updated content, by writing a blog, by leaving insightful comments on other people's blogs, by having articles written about you, and by updating your websites and your social profiles.

Remember that the internet has a mind like a steel trap – it will not forget. That innocent comment that you left on a blog that could be misinterpreted if read out of context? It will most likely be indexed and found if a customer searches for your name to learn more about you. Be careful what you say – everything is public.

🔊 **New, updated content is key.** Make a commitment to update your social profiles, do a few blog entries a week, upload new information to your website (for instance, new customers, new messages about availability, updates on what you are working on), publish articles in online newsletters (www.eHow.com, www.knol.google.com or other online platforms), etc. This is a never-ending project, and you will not achieve a high ranking in a day. The internet essentially rewards hard work, and with few exceptions you get out of it what you put into it.

🔊 **Create relevant content about yourself and place it where it will be seen.** Blogs, Twitter, LinkedIn, and Xing are your friends. And they are jealous friends, so keep them happy by feeding them new content.

🔊 **Do not overdo it.** If you do not have anything to say, do not say it. Be careful not to dilute your brand, especially with press releases, by sending out irrelevant or unimportant information too frequently. Also, do not register for 50 social and professional profiles that you cannot maintain. Keep it interesting and fresh, and start small with only a few profiles and a limited online footprint.

🔊 **Yes, do it: search for yourself and see where you rank.** While it is certainly narcissistic, you have a legitimate business reason to Google yourself. Search for your name, or better, search for 'translator + your language pair + city' and see where you rank. Are you on the first two pages? Do this often, but do not be surprised if one day you are on page one and the next on page ten: the algorithms are a mystery. If you search for your name, it will give you a good idea which tools are working: check which sites come up first if you search for your name and keep on investing time into them.

🔊 **Develop keywords and integrate them into your HTML code and text.** If you do not know which keywords to use, there are some excellent tools for keyword research. The Google Adwords keyword tool (https://adwords.google.com/select/KeywordToolExternal is remarkably good at finding related keywords and phrases for you. The second tool is the free research tool from Wordtracker (http://freekeywords.wordtracker.com). Last but not least, there is KeywordIndex, (www.keywordindex.com), a new online keyword suggestion tool that helps you to find good keywords for your website. It is available in English and in German. If you have found the right keywords to describe your services, put them into the meta title of your page and into the body of your page. But make sure you do not overload the page with keywords, which makes it difficult to read. Your customers are human and you should create a well-written, easy-to-read text, including occasional keywords where they make sense. Do not become obsessed with constantly tweaking title tags, headings, and on-page content. For more in-advice, visit www.highrankings.com, which focuses on how to write for search engines and your customers.

🐾 **Do not cheat the system.** You will get penalized for duplicate content. Search engines are smart enough to recognize if someone buys two domain names, such as www.spanishwizards.com and www.spanishwizardusa.com and puts the exact same content on both sites, hoping to score a higher ranking. Most likely, the search engines will penalize you by not ranking one or both of your sites, so play fair. If you have several websites, a good rule of thumb is to make sure that at least 60% of the content is different between the sites, and that does not mean just changing the syntax. You can also create a redirect from www.spanishwizardusa.com to www. spanishwizards.com, which will not get you penalized.

🐾 **Take it in stride.** SEO is very important, but you also have to continue to build your reputation far away from search engines, in something as traditional as – gasp! – conversations, meetings, e-mails, phone calls, and so on. Once your potential client knows your name and/or your company name, you will not need to worry about search engine optimization. If you have a catchy business name, if you have handed out enough business cards, if you generate enough word of mouth, people will already know where to find you. Look at SEO as the online version of traditional networking on steroids, but do not forget the basics.[8]

No free e-mail addresses

As an entrepreneur, you should have a professional e-mail address associated with your domain name. Relying on a free e-mail address is not quite appropriate in the business world. Put yourself in the customer's shoes. How seriously do you take vendors who contact you about their services from a Hotmail or Gmail address? These addresses typically lead potential customers to think one of more of the following:

🐾 **You are not a serious business.** Worst-case scenario: someone would think you message is scam and delete the e-mail without even reading it.

---

8   Judy Jenner, "Basic SEO for linguists," ITI Bulletin (January - February 2010): 16-17. Article has been shortened and adapted to fit the format of this book. Reprinted with permission of the ITI Bulletin.

You are not running a very professional business. We all know that a serious website does not necessarily equal a serious business. However, in the 21st century, having an e-mail address at a paid domain name really is a basic requirement for running a business.

You have not put a lot of thought or effort into your business. While that is most likely not the case, what matters is your potential customers' perception.

Get organized

When doing a marketing/advertising campaign, or simply during the regular course of business, you will be sending a lot of e-mail and potentially snail mail. You might think you remember whom you sent what, but chances are you will not. Why rely on your memory when you can use computing tools to make your life easier? Being highly organized and being able to locate files and correspondence will make you a better businessperson and save you time and money, not to mention headaches: no more feelings of I-know-I-put-it-somewhere-and-now-I-cannot-find-it.

The beauty of blind copying

Your first order of business should be blind-copying yourself on relevant outgoing communication with clients and potential clients. This is not necessary for every message you send, but is quite essential for important messages of which you would like to have a record. Knowing how the conversation with your customer or prospect has progressed (rates, details, etc.) will allow you to easily reconstruct the transaction in question. In addition, it will give you a solid written record should any dispute arise. For instance, we blind-copy ourselves on all price quotes or contacts with new customers. Then we move those e-mails to a "potential customer" archive folder on our e-mail directory structure. You can further categorize this folder by having sub-folders for each potential client if you would like.

E-mail folders and archiving

Having your e-mail under control is a significant part of being organized. We suggest starting by taking a hard look at which e-mails you want to keep. It is tempting to save forwarded messages or your cousin's wedding pictures, but you are better off deleting the former and saving the latter on your hard drive. Many of us strive to move toward a paperless office, which is a lofty and worthwhile goal. Now we face another kind of overwhelming task: an immense amount of virtual paper. Data cleaning means getting rid of items and files you do not want, just like you would do if you were to go through your desk. If an e-mail has been in your inbox for several months, and you have not done anything with it, hit the delete button. For everything else, create a folder. You should separate personal correspondence from business correspondence. Some of the business folders can then be divided by potential customers, existing customers with subfolders for each customer, speaking engagements at conferences with subfolders for each organization, newsletter submissions, translation resources, SEO, fellow translators, translation blogs, local translation organization, etc. Also create cleverly named "Miscellaneous" and "Pending" folders. Do not create too many folders, as you want to avoid having an unmanageable amount of folders. We have found that having a few different subfolders greatly increases our chances of finding an item. If you spend more than two or three minutes looking for a particular e-mail, you have done a poor job at getting organized. You can also save attachments that are sent to you via e-mail on your hard drive folder structure and then delete the e-mail.

The volume of e-mail and overwhelming amount of data can be further complicated if you have more than one address set up on your e-mail client. There are different ways of handling this, but we only have one set of e-mail folders and archives, to which we move e-mails from all different accounts. Our goal is to have an inbox that is empty except for e-mails that are pending that we need to address.

Another good option is to archive old e-mails. You could create an archive yearly or at any other interval that works for you. For detailed instructions on how to accomplish this in Microsoft Outlook, please visit http://office.microsoft.com/en-us/outlook/HA011216101033.aspx and for Mozilla Thunderbird instructions, please visit http://kb.mozillazine.org/Archiving_your_e-mail.

The folder system for e-mail is also a good strategy to apply to all the virtual documents on your hard drive.

E-mail filters

Our IT guru, Thomas Gruber, recommended using e-mail filters to us a few years ago. It saves a significant amount of time and effort and is very easy to set up. Check your e-mail client's options, where you will find a "filter" or "rules" option. Here, depending on how your e-mail client is configured, you will be able to select how you would like your e-mails to be filtered. In other words, you can specify certain keywords, subjects, or senders to go directly into pre-defined folders, thus bypassing your inbox and preventing it from becoming cluttered. For instance, listservs can be quite active and generate a substantial amount of e-mail. We enjoy reading them and responding to questions, but we send them directly to a folder and just look at it a few times a day. We configured our e-mail client so that any messages with "newsgroup" in the sender's address go directly into the "newsgroup" folders. This comes in really handy, especially if you subscribe to several newsgroups. Sending e-mail directly to folders is also a great idea to help send potential junk mail directly into the trash, including domain names from which you know that they can produce no interesting messages. Having these filters has saved us a lot of time, so go ahead and spend five minutes setting them up.

The pitching process

Many freelance writers will tell you that pitching to editors to buy their stories (for print publications) is quite an art. While as linguists we are not pitching to editors, but mostly to executives in communications, marketing, or advertising, the strategies are quite similar. This part of the marketing process requires some thought and insight, and is an effort that never really ends.

Whom to pitch to

This is perhaps the most important part of the pitching process. The only resource you have is your time, and you need to allocate it smartly. It is always much better to get introduced to someone than to approach them without a common connection (which we previously discussed in the cold calling section). However, it will not always be possible to find a common connection who can introduce you to your prospect. If you decide to approach prospects without having qualified the lead first, you should put some thought into whom you want to approach. You should narrow the field of people you want to pitch to using the following criteria:

Specialization. Does the person you are trying to pitch to work in an area in which you have demonstrated expertise?

Geography. Self-employed linguists can work globally, which is fantastic. However, if you live in a metropolitan market where there are enough businesses in your field, consider finding local companies to pitch to, as you might have an advantage over someone from out of town. Be sure to highlight that you are a local vendor with good knowledge of the market, if applicable. Ask if you could arrange a brief meeting to tell the prospect about your services.

Contact person. Consider pitching to an executive in communications, advertising, marketing, or public relations, since these departments tend to handle translations. There are exceptions to that rule, and sometimes it can be challenging to figure out who is in charge of outsourcing language services. It could be an executive assistant who has been tasked with finding a freelance translator, especially if the company has never worked with linguists before and needs a one-off translation. If you already know that your new contact is in charge of translation vendor management, then you should customize your pitch to that person's knowledge of the languages industry, which might be more substantial than that of someone who has no experience working with linguists.

&. The company's financial situation. You do not want to pitch to a company that has just announced that it is putting a hold on its international business expansion for the indefinite future. Do your homework before you approach any company and read literature relevant to their industries and businesses.

E-mail pitch

In today's fast-paced world, many people prefer the quick response (and eco-friendliness) of e-mail. It is cheap and fast, and it helps save the planet. This is not to discourage anyone from sending traditional letters, which seem to be more effective in Europe than in the U.S. They can be a valuable and effective marketing strategy. However, many times, they do not make it to the intended person's desk and could be disposed of by an assistant. While many assistants also screen executives' e-mails for items they do not need to read, in general, your chances of getting through to the intended person are higher once you have their e-mail address. Here are some good guidelines to follow.

&. **Always address the person by his or her name**. "Dear executive," "Dear Sir," and "To whom it may concern" are not acceptable. Nothing gets us to hit the "delete" button quicker than an impersonal greeting. It shows that you have not researched the company, do not know if the contact person is male or female. The message also clearly says that you want to take up the recipient's time while not bothering to invest time yourself. This is not a good start to a potential business relationship, so it must be avoided at all cost. We routinely get e-mails addressed to "Dear Sirs." If the person looked on our website, he or she would quickly figure out that we are a women-owned business. We suggest addressing the person by his or her first name (or last name, if you want to be more formal) in the U.S. and by their last name in most other countries. In addition, when using pronouns, you need to go to great lengths to find out whether your contact person is male or female, which can be quite challenging in the U.S. with names such as Alex, Shannon, Chris, Casey, Jackie, Leslie, Terry, etc. Luckily, in writing, there are many ways to get around pronouns, which is not the case over the phone. Be prepared. Do a quick online search on your contact person and hope there is an image on the LinkedIn profile or some news article that refers to the person's gender. When in doubt, research.

Be relevant and specific. Tell your prospect, in three paragraphs or less, who you are and what you can do for them. Avoid starting with "My name is…." The recipient can see your name from the e-mail address and your e-mail signature. Writing "I understand that you are opening a new office in Madrid, and would like to meet with you regarding the translation of all your company materials into top-notch Spanish" is a good, specific way to tell the contact person what you are all about.

Be short. It is safe to assume that all your prospects are busy and that their inboxes are flooded with hundreds of e-mails every day, just like yours. Keep your information to a minimum. No one wants to read a half-page introductory e-mail message.

PDF attachment. Your e-mail should include your company profile attached as a PDF file. It should be no more than two pages long, and ideally a single page. Most direct clients are not inherently familiar with the details of our industry and our businesses, so do not tell them what version of a specific translation memory tool you use. Keep it simple and ask yourself: if you were a customer about to buy translation or interpretation services, and you had no insight into the business, what would you want to know?

Offer solutions. Wanting to sell your potential customer your services is perfectly legitimate, but think about what solutions you are really offering. Do not leave it to the client to figure out how they could possibly use your services. Identify a potential problem, which could include previous poor translations, lack of presence in a certain market, documented problems the company has had because of lack of bilingual materials, etc. Do not say: "Please let me know if there is anything I can do for you." Say: "I would like to meet with you and discuss my proposal on how you can best take advantage of the emerging Asian market by opening a distribution center in Shanghai, as your CEO has suggested. I have the tools and the knowledge to localize your website."

🔖 **Integrate feedback.** Most companies, unless you have been introduced to someone directly, will not take the time to tell you the reason they are not interested in your services. In the rare case that they do, use that information and integrate it into your pitch process. Do not take it personally and thank the writer for their feedback. Constructive criticism – as challenging as it can sometimes be – is a great way to improve. Consider asking a friend or colleague to review your materials and to give you feedback.

Buying ads

While incurring marketing and advertising expenses upfront without any guaranteed return on investment is difficult, you should be making small investments in your professional future. Years ago, a friend suggested we spend $10,000 for advertising in our first year. He meant well, but needless to say, we spent a fraction of what he suggested, and we try to spend it where it will have the most impact. Again, you cannot predict what will do well, but before you take out an ad anywhere, look at the circulation, who the readers are and where it will be distributed. Most importantly: have a strategy before you start spending the money. Ask yourself this question: would a potential client in my area of specialization read this? You are making educated guesses, so your best bet is to take out ads in narrow fields. For instance, if you do a lot of automotive translation, you should look at advertising in a magazine or trade journal that is read by folks on the marketing and communication side of the auto industry. Chances are you know which magazines those are, because you probably already read them to stay abreast of what is happening in your industry. If you do a lot of personal document translation, consider taking out an ad in the student newspaper of your university or a small, community-based newspaper (ads in large newspapers are usually prohibitively expensive). If you focus on legal translation, consider taking out a small ad in a local legal journal, which can be fairly inexpensive. Are you an audiovisual translator? How about taking out an ad with your local film office? Put some thought into how you can best use your limited funds.

How to spend $100

Here is an example of how to spend your (fictional) $100 yearly marketing and advertising budget.

🔖 **$10.** The best use you can make of $10 is to purchase the domain name of your website. See the website section of this chapter for detailed instructions on how to get your own website with Google Sites.

≈ **$20.** Spend around $20 at your local copy shop or online printing service to make marketing flyers that will serve as your main marketing materials. These can be tri-folds, one-page flyers, or two-sided documents. Try to stay away from color copies, as they are more expensive, and maximize your investment and consider black and white print on tasteful colored paper.

≈ **$30.** For roughly $30, you can get around 500 high-quality business cards (cost varies depending on the number of colors, the type of finish, etc.) You should not leave home without having your business cards on you, so this is the best small investment you can make. You do not want to be the person who runs out of business cards at a meeting or networking event, so order ahead if you are about to run out.

≈ **$40.** Consider spending $40 on relevant ads in very targeted, specific publications and newsletters. Look for specialty publications that are in your area of specialization. Do not focus on large dailies and weeklies, since the cost of advertising there is usually quite prohibitive for small businesses.

CHAPTER 5

೩.

BUSINESS DEVELOPMENT

Our translation and interpretation work focuses entirely on direct clients. Working with direct clients instead of translation agencies is traditionally more lucrative and allows for more flexibility. In addition, it typically increases linguists' quality of life because there is generally less time pressure for turnaround, which hence gives us more control over our time and businesses. Being an integral part of direct clients' international marketing strategy makes translation work more rewarding, both financially and professionally. Challenges of working with direct clients include a potentially long and time-consuming customer acquisition process and finding the time, motivation, and strategy to pursue this type of customer for the first time. However, any linguist can shift from working mainly for agencies to working with direct clients if they approach the process in an organized and targeted fashion and are willing to put hard work into it.

Many of our colleagues would like to have more direct clients and work with fewer agencies. Other colleagues enjoy the straightforward, low-effort interaction with agencies and the fact that they do not have to do any of the marketing or business development. Both approaches and hybrid versions work well for different people. At its most basic, the choice between translation agencies and direct clients can be exemplified by a revenue versus effort equation. If you work with direct customers, you will be able to charge a higher rate. However, finding direct customers will be infinitely more work than accepting projects from agencies. Thus, you will probably work on fewer projects, especially in the beginning. You can charge higher rates when you work with direct customers because the intermediary is taken out of the equation. Many corporations prefer to work with large translation agencies so they only have to deal with one vendor for multiple languages. On the flipside, other corporations like working with very small businesses because of the uncomplicated interaction and lack of red tape. It is your job to convince the direct client that they should work with you.

Direct-customer acquisition strategies

"How do I find direct clients?" is the question that we are asked most often, and it really is the million-dollar question. Before you begin to think about where to find direct clients, you need to spend time developing a plan, a strategy, and some marketing ideas. Please read the marketing chapter, decide what your competitive advantage is, and identify the business areas you would like to work in. Without these crucial first steps you will not be successful in attracting direct clients. The basis for finding clients in our business is the same as it is in any business: networking and meeting people. It is how attorneys, doctors, financial advisors, and real estate agents grow their businesses, and linguists need to do the same thing. Some of the ideas we have outlined below are very strongly correlated to the strategies we mention in the marketing chapter.

If you do not have a plan, your potential customers will notice. You cannot target the market as a whole, and you need to find one or several fields to focus on. You do not want to be the person at a networking function who says to a potential client "I translate in all areas." It makes you look unfocused and unprofessional, akin to a lawyer who practices in all areas of the law.

Many times, linguists think that business will magically come to them if they buy an ad or have a website. In today's crowded marketplace, that will not be the case. Think about it this way: you have to be proactive instead of reactive when it comes to getting business. Tens of thousands of sales books have been written on this process, but we will keep it simple. Like most linguists, we are not natural salespeople, so think of it as business development and marketing rather than sales.

First things first

You need to have a strategy before you can even think about starting the direct client customer acquisition process. Here are some issues you need to think about.

- Which companies/industries/sectors do you want to target?

- Where can you find these individuals or these companies?

- Do you already have contacts in this industry?

- Where are the industry-specific events?

- Can you join a relevant trade group?

- Can you ask a contact to take you to an event attended by people in your target group?

- Can you buy low-cost advertising in an industry-specific publication?

- Are you up-to-date with what is happening in the particular industry or sector that you want to translate or interpret for?

No pain, no gain

Do you think it is intimidating to approach a potential client at a mixer at your local chamber of commerce? Yes? How about walking into a tradeshow full of sharply dressed, busy professionals you have never met? Does that make you nervous? It makes us feel that way, too. If the thought of doing this causes you to lose sleep and/or have nightmares, perhaps this strategy is not for you. However, if you are experiencing mild discomfort at the thought of moving outside of your comfort zone – which is more than normal – then you should give this strategy a try, especially if you have found that you have come to a halt in your new client acquisition strategy. If you are not happy with your current strategy and/or your current results, you need to make some changes. This will mean confronting some situations and dealing with things that you are, perhaps, not used to, but you will learn, grow, and succeed; even if it is not the first time around. Get used to the idea that the direct client acquisition strategy, like everything in life, will be quite challenging and complex when you try it for the first time. The old cliché, however, does apply: it will get easier and it will get better if you spend time and energy on growing and learning. Approaching your second potential client at a tradeshow will be much easier than approaching your first one.

If you expect this process to be easy, then stop reading now. You will be building the customer base for your business and that is quite difficult. If you like the comfort of turning on the computer in the morning and having several projects from agencies waiting for you, then perhaps the direct client strategy is not for you. If you are not willing to work hard, deal with some disappointments, and invest time into building your core of customers, then this is not for you. If you expect immediate results, then this is not for you. If you think there is a magic wand, then this is not for you. Ready?

Yes, you can

We hear this frequently: "I want to find direct customers but it is too much work." If working with direct customers were both easy (it is not) and very lucrative (which it is), everyone would be doing it. Here are a few potential reasons for opting not to work with direct clients we have heard throughout the years, and all of them are valid. If you find yourself nodding in agreement with all these statements, then perhaps you are not ready to move into direct customer territory. If you find that a few of these statements apply to you, but that you are willing to work on them, then we suggest you give it a try.

- It is too much work.

- I am too busy.

- I already have enough work.

- Direct customers are too demanding.

- I am shy.

- I do not like going to networking events.

- I do not have any creative marketing ideas.

- I do not know where to start.

All of these statements include things that you can work on, including shyness. You will make the time if you really want to pursue this strategy, and you will find that most direct customers have reasonable expectations. Marketing ideas will come with time, and you can work with friends to help you brainstorm. After reading this book, you should know where to start.

Go where the clients are

While it is very important that you go to professional development events that focus on translation or interpretation to improve your skills and network with your colleagues, it is also critical that you attend events where your clients will be. Determining what events these are will take some research and trial and error. Before you can make the determination, you have to know who you are targeting, which brings us back to the marketing chapter. For instance, if your area of specialization is public relations, a part of your customer base might be composed of public relations agencies. Those agencies and their employees will tend to attend industry-specific events, such as meetings of public relations associations. It is there that you will be able to make valuable contacts. Some of these meetings and networking events might be restricted to professionals in the field, but many are open to anyone. Depending on the event, there might be a fee involved. There is nothing wrong with going to a networking event to sell your services. In fact, that is what these types of events are for. It might be intimidating to walk into a room full of people you do not know with the objective of promoting your services. If the thought of this frightens you, team up with a colleague, either in the same field or someone who offers a completely different service. If you are still anxious, go to a mixer or other event without the goal of talking to anyone – just soak in the atmosphere, look around, and get comfortable with your surroundings. Perhaps the next time you go you will be ready to make some contacts. Many of us are introverts, so do not be too hard on yourself if you feel like a fish out of water. These events will become easier and more routine the more you go to them. In terms of the contacts you make, what matters is the quality of the contacts, not the quantity. Walking away with a large stack of business cards is not necessarily a good thing.

Be known as someone who offers solutions

When you meet a potential client and get a business card, take time to research the company before you send a proposal or information about your services. The more you know about your potential client's company, the better. Show that you are informed and offer a solution to a potential language problem that your potential client did not even know she had. Word will spread quickly that you are someone who is thoughtful about where you services might fit in instead of just saying to potential clients: "Let me know if there is any work for me."

Meet more people

The only way to get more clients is to meet more people, both online and offline. You need to combine these two strategies in order to continuously grow your circle and the number of people who know about you. The offline strategy will include moving out of your comfort zone and your familiar home office and to network, network, network. While any one person you meet might not need your services, perhaps that person's brother-in-law does. Once your name is out in the community, hopefully it will be on the tip of potential clients' tongues. The person you met at the mixer a few weeks ago might tell his contacts that he recently met a very professional language service provider. You never know what opportunities are out there for you, and if you do not try to make contacts, you will never know. You might be quite surprised by the wealth of translation and interpretation opportunities that exist, including things you never would have considered or thought of. And success breeds success, so keep at it.

Get creative

Just because it has not been done before does not mean a strategy cannot be successful. If you come up with a creative idea for meeting potential clients, implement it. If you translate mainly in the hospitality industry, why not put together a small glossary of food terms in your language to distribute at an industry event? It might serve as a nice icebreaker, and if you provide something of value to attendees, organizers might consider letting you address the audience. Be memorable, and be short and sweet. The creative ideas that work for you will depend very strongly on your competitive advantage, your strengths and weaknesses, where you live, and your specialization.

Keep an open mind

When you start your quest for direct customers, it is important to constantly think about your business. When you are reading the newspaper, always keep your business in mind and think about the possibilities that you can read and learn about. For instance, if you are an interpreter and you have read that the local welfare office had to lay off its full-time interpreters, perhaps now is the time to offer your contract services. If you were made aware through a colleague that construction companies are now required by law to provide additional hazard training to their employees, that might be a good opportunity to translate educational materials into other languages. Once you start thinking like a business owner, a lot of ideas will come to you. Write them down immediately so you do not forget them. Time permitting, research and implement your ideas.

Change your attitude

Many colleagues are often disappointed by individual mixers, events, or meetings they attend. They are discouraged when they do not see an immediate return on their investment, that is, their time. While not getting business is disheartening, it is analogous to complaining about not getting customers the very first day you buy an ad in a newspaper. It is all about repetition and reinforcement, and business will come if you make yourself known and keep promoting your services. Do not stop your networking efforts if you leave the chamber of commerce without a signed contract for a two-month project. Expecting to get that sort of response is unrealistic. There are no guarantees: just hard work.

Have clients come to you

In addition to seeking out clients, which will be a substantial part of your strategy, think about how you can get them to come to you. The first strategy that comes to mind is advertising, but that is typically quite costly. Let us focus on free ways to do this. The best way is to get profiled in local, regional, national, or even international media. This is a time-consuming project, but it will not cost you a penny beyond the cost of your time. Develop a pitch to editors of magazines or business newspapers. Please see the marketing chapter for more information on this process. Try your university alumni newsletter, even if you no longer live in the area. Another great way to get free publicity is to win an award. If you have done a good job at promoting your services and once people know you have great services to offer, you might be lucky enough to be nominated for a small business or other type of award. If you hear about an award that you might qualify for but are not nominated, it is perfectly reasonable to ask a trusted business connection if she would be willing to nominate you.

No secrets

We are frequently asked to share our secrets. Last year, a reporter asked Judy if she was afraid of sharing her secrets. The answer is that there are really no secrets, and that everyone's strategies will be quite specific to their skills and competitive advantage. Some strategies are universal, and we are delighted to share them. Perhaps the not-so-secret secret is that you need to create a solid plan and execute it in a methodical manner.

Pre-qualified contacts

This is something we addressed in detail in the marketing chapter under "the art of getting introduced." Remember that the chances of getting business when cold-calling are very low. If you are not busy on a given day and want to spend a few hours on this, try e-mailing or calling people with whom you do not share a contact. If you do have a contact in common, the person you are trying to reach will be much more inclined to talk to you. Think of yourself as a customer: how many e-mails from complete strangers do you read? On the other hand, if the e-mail comes from one of your contacts, or the contact's name is referenced in the subject line, you are typically much more likely to open it, correct? The same holds true for your customers. They want to know, before they even have a conversation with you, that you are a trustworthy individual. Establishing those kinds of pre-qualified leads is the best way to build your business. While it is a lot more difficult than opening the phone book and making random phone calls, it also has a much higher success rate, is more professional, more targeted, and will be more rewarding in both the short and the long run.

However, you will not be able to find a common connection with everyone you want to approach. For instance: You find a company on LinkedIn or another professional networking site that works in precisely your area, say, designing Belgian lace. You have a background in Belgian lace design, and you have researched this company, which is based in Belgium, and they are trying to export to the U.S., where you live. Your translation specialization is textiles. While you do not have a contact at this company, you have done your homework and you are able to offer solutions and customized services to this company. It is perfectly fine to e-mail the company, tell them about your background, and detail how you can help them achieve their sales goals in the U.S. Make your subject line catchy and memorable, for instance: "French->English translator and Belgian lace expert will help you achieve your export goals" or something similar.

Pro bono work

Pro bono work, that is, work that is performed without financial compensation, is, not surprisingly, not always popular. However, sometimes you need to give before you can get (also see our chapter on giving back), and that is not limited to volunteer work within the translation industry. Consider this: pro bono opportunities might come your way that could get you closer to a potential client you have wanted to contact for some time. Other times, pro bono work might appear to have no possible benefit for you, but you never know what it could lead to. If the time commitment is reasonable and the event is local, our recommendation is to carve out some time for the occasional pro bono job. For instance, you might give a free presentation about your job at a high school career day. Next thing you know, the principal might contact you about translations for non-English speaking parents. Or you might volunteer during a fundraiser by requesting donated items for the auction. While this is tedious and time-consuming work, your name will get out in the community, and you will build some goodwill for both yourself and your business. List your volunteer activities on your website and perhaps on your marketing materials if they are relevant. You might even receive an invite to the high-end fundraiser that you volunteered for, and end up sharing the table with a group of highly successful people. Talk always tends to revolve around work, and it is a great opportunity to talk about both your pro bono work and your real job. More often than not, people will remember you if they sat at your table and you made an impression. The next time they or someone in their circle of business associates needs a language services professional, they might think of you. There are no guarantees, but it is worth the effort.

The business card approach

This one is quite simple, inexpensive, and often quite effective. It simply entails never leaving home without business cards. It does not matter if you are driving down the street to pick up milk at the store, just dropping off your kid at school, or heading to the dog park on a Saturday. The best salespeople will tell you that they are always prepared, no matter where they go. Interesting conversations can happen almost anywhere, and frequently you will get asked what you do for a living, especially if you reside in the United States. When you mention what you do, there is no need to immediately distribute business cards, but develop a sixth sense as to whether the person you are talking to wants your information or not. There is really no excuse not to have business cards on you – they weigh almost nothing and are easy to carry around. You do not want to be among the people who head to mixers and conferences and run out of business cards. Order ahead, and bring 100 more than you think you might need. The more of your business cards are in circulation in professional and social circles, the better. We have actually won new clients that we have met at baby showers, at happy hours, and while playing tennis.

Resource allocation

As an entrepreneur, your time is the only resource you have, so use it wisely. Most likely, you will be the only person working at your company, which means you wear many hats, including director of marketing, director of business development, collections agent, accounting supervisor, systems administrator, and head of community relations. Deciding how to spend your time is not always an easy task, but to help you make these decisions, remember that every event that you commit to comes with an opportunity cost. For instance, when you go to a networking mixer, you might lose about three hours of translation time. During this time, you could have made a certain amount of money translating. That is your opportunity cost. Even if you did not have a project lined up, you could have gone to the gym, recharged your batteries while taking a nap, or spent time with a loved one. The bottom line is that since there is a cost for everything, you need to work on saying no to things that do not interest you or that you do not think are valuable for your business. It is challenging to turn people down, but you will need to pick and choose wisely in order to be successful. There is some trial and error involved, and it is more art than science, but take a hard look at which activities you are doing and why.

The tradeshow approach

The prevailing wisdom is that tradeshows are a fantastic way to find direct customers. We agree, but this is easier in the tradeshow capital of the world, Las Vegas, then in Crested Butte, Colorado. While larger cities host a significant amount of conventions and tradeshows, those linguists who live in rural areas or smaller towns will be at a disadvantage. However, those colleagues could consider planning an entire business trip to a tradeshow or convention to advertise their services. Most of the costs incurred during a trip of this nature are considered business expenses, and can be deducted from your business taxes. Please check with your tax professional for details.

Tradeshow advice

Going to tradeshows is an effective strategy for finding direct clients. You should, however, be aware that the experience might be a bit painful, especially if you are not an extrovert. There is a reason that sales floors are full of very extroverted, highly social people. Humanities people do not always fall into that group, and that is fine. You do not have to be a natural salesperson to pitch your services at a convention, but it certainly helps. Introverts can succeed too, but it will be more of a challenge.

The first question is: how will you find out about tradeshows? If you live in a major city, you can sign up for an RSS feed from your local convention and visitors authority. This way, you will receive a regular update of the upcoming conventions and tradeshows. Alternatively, check if your chamber of commerce lists upcoming events. Most of these events are booked at least a year in advance, so you should have no problem putting them on your schedule and working around them with plenty of time to prepare.

Your real homework starts right after you have identified the event you wish to attend. There are several considerations, mainly cost. Most of these events are quite large and are targeted at companies that can afford to pay tens of thousands of dollars for a booth. Many times there are more affordable passes available that only include entry to the expo floor, which is where you want to focus your attention. These passes typically exclude entry into educational sessions or mixers. Check the event's website for the prices. Some are not open to the public, and some require that you do actual business in that industry. For many large tradeshows with tens of thousands of attendees, just gaining access to the expo might be expensive. However, smaller events often offer free access to the expo floor in the hopes of attracting more visitors and increasing the size of the event. It is also quite possible that tradeshow organizers want to discourage the general public, which could include potential vendors, from attending. After all, the folks who have bought these expensive booths are looking to sell their product or service, and might not necessarily be receptive potential buyers. A good piece of advice for gaining entry into tradeshow halls is to check if your local convention center is looking for volunteers. There might be a need for volunteers for a specific event, which could include greeting visitors, giving them information about the city, or directing traffic. While you will not get paid for your time, you will most likely get access to the conference/tradeshow in exchange for your services. Make sure that you keep your volunteering and your marketing efforts separate. Wait until your volunteering assignment is complete before you start approaching vendors and attendees with your business proposition.

🍃 **Try to get free admission to the tradeshow.** Take a look at all your contacts, online and offline, and find companies that are in the tradeshow's line of business. Then verify that they will actually participate in the tradeshow. You can easily check this by looking at the online exhibitors listing. Next, approach your contacts, preferably the ones you know well, and inquire whether the company has some guest passes for the conference. Simply explain your intentions – there is absolutely nothing wrong with trying to grow your business. Ask a few of your contacts the same question. If you do get a pass, take your contact person for lunch or dinner. Also, if your contact is giving you the pass, consider asking him or her if they would be willing to introduce you to a few people at the show. Be sure to not take up too much of anyone's time: tradeshows are a very busy time for most companies, especially if they have their own booth.

🍃 **Research the vendors.** It is not very time-effective to simply go to the show, wander around, and approach random booths. It will not make you look very professional, and it is not the best use of your time. Preparing for these events can be time-consuming, but it will be worth it once you are at the event. Look at the exhibitor list and pick 20 or so companies that you would like to approach. Then research them in detail. Where are they headquartered? Do they have an international presence? Do they want one? Do they have multilingual websites, and if they do, could they be improved? After you finish all your research, you should have a short, but highly targeted, list of companies you would like to speak to.

Tradeshow checklist

Now that you have identified and researched the companies you would like to have conversations with, you need a targeted approach to ensure that you get a meeting.

🍃 As we discussed in the marketing chapter, you need to **develop customized marketing proposals and materials** for each potential client you approach. In your marketing materials and/or proposal, outline what you can do for the company, how you fit into their long-term goals, and why they should hire you. Show your potential client that you have put some thought into how you can help them achieve their goals. Be a problem-solver with a plan, not strictly a salesperson.

🍃 **Think about the best time to go.** Tradeshows are busy times for both exhibitors and attendees. It is possible that the person you are trying to make contact with is an attendee, an exhibitor, a speaker, or all of these things. If you know that he or she is a speaker, attend his or her session. If you know that your contact person will be at the booth all day, consider taking him or her for a coffee break. The more you know about the other person's schedule, the better. If you do not have that information, do not assume anything and simply offer options. If they tell you that now is not a good time, ask what time would be better. Take a look at the tradeshow or convention schedule and identify slower times. For example, the tradeshow floor might be less busy if there are several educational sessions or workshops going on simultaneously. Take advantage of these times, as you might get more face-to-face time with the people you would like to approach. Standing in line to talk to someone is not the best use of your time.

Who does not like donuts or, even better, a nutritious snack? If you have attended tradeshows before, you will have noticed that they traditionally feature snack booths with overpriced, poor-quality food. Many exhibitors and attendees are too busy to leave the convention area during the day to have a healthy (or at least good) snack. Solve this problem for them by bringing some easy-to-transport food with you and offer to leave it for the entire team. Give it a try and do not forget to log the cost as a business expense. This strategy works best when you bring goodies to vendors with whom you have already made appointments; it would not be cost-effective for you to distribute donuts everywhere.

Bring small promotional items. Put some thought into this, try to make it translation or interpretation specific, and stay away from the obvious: pens, mousepads, laser pointers – we all have too many of these already. Our favorite potential customer gift is the USB stick embedded in a beautiful, hand-painted, miniature traditional Dutch shoe that we described in the relationship building section of the marketing chapter.

Try to pre-schedule meetings. Depending on the tradeshow, you might be able to pre-set meetings with exhibitors prior to the event. You will most likely only have access to this feature if you are registered as a full attendee, which might be expensive. If this option is available to you, try to pre-arrange as many meetings as possible. If you do not have access to this system, identify the individuals you would like to meet by looking at the exhibitor list, and consult your networks to see if you and the person you would like to get in touch with share an acquaintance. Then ask for an introduction and pre-arrange a meeting. This way, you will already have pre-qualified the potential sales lead, making the interaction at the show less stressful. While you can simply e-mail the person you want to approach without having a connection, this strategy traditionally has quite a low success rate. However, if you have some extra time on your hands, you should give it a try.

🐾 **Learn when to walk away.** If someone has made it clear to you that they are not interested in your services, politely leave a business card, thank the person for their time, and move on. If you catch yourself starting sentences with "but," then you are unconsciously applying used car salesmen or tele-marketer principles, which will quickly earn you a bad reputation.

🐾 **Follow up.** If a person has expressed interest in your services, follow up with them in a week. Be aware that most people will be quite busy after a weeklong tradeshow, and that they might not respond as quickly as you would hope. Be patient, and include something along the lines of "Follow-Up: XYZ Tradeshow from XYZ" in your e-mail subject line.

🐾 **Write thank-you notes.** If someone has taken quite a bit of time to talk to you and is interested in potentially doing business with you, send an e-mail thank-you note. Be sincere and make sure your message does not come across as yet another marketing strategy. Do not send it unless you really mean it, and stay away from hyperbole in your text. Sending thank-you notes is more common in the U.S. than in other countries, so make sure that it is culturally appropriate to do so in the country you live in.

🐾 **Get your own booth.** At large tradeshows, getting your own booth as a solo language services provider is traditionally cost-prohibitive. However, most cities have smaller shows and events through chambers of commerce, small business development agencies, entrepreneurship associations, etc. These booths are usually just basic tables and are quite affordable. If your local translation and interpretation association has a presence at the event, offer to help staff the table. However, be aware that you are representing the association, not yourself. That does not mean that you are barred from handing out your own business cards, but be mindful of your role.

Case study: direct client acquisition

The following step-by-step case study should help you understand the direct client acquisition process even better. Keep in mind that this process can take quite a bit of time. The following case study is an example from our own practice. For confidentiality reasons, we will refer to the client only as "the company."

🐾 **Do your homework.** While we have several clients in the Las Vegas gaming business, there are still a lot of companies that have a presence in Spanish-speaking gaming markets that are not our clients (yet). We wanted to acquire more customers in the gaming industry. We researched the five largest companies and took a look at their international marketing strategies and their goals in the overseas markets.

❧ Read applicable industry journals. We read gaming-specific publications and the gaming sections of Las Vegas newspapers and magazines, which widely cover the gaming industry. We narrowed our search down to three companies.

❧ Find the right contact. Once we had determined the companies we wanted to focus on, we started the task of finding contacts that we had within the companies. Off the top of our heads, we had no contacts, but we reviewed our connections on professional networking sites, such as LinkedIn, and found that the person we wanted to talk to at "the company" – we will call her Jane – was a connection of a close friend of ours, Joe, who works for a different company.

❧ Ask for the introduction without being pushy. We approached Joe, told him about our business development efforts, and inquired how well he knew Jane. He knew her on a professional level and had lunch with her once in a while. Joe was gracious enough to make an e-mail introduction and let us take it from there. He drafted a quick message to Jane, on which he copied us, informing her of our background and that we had found that her company had a need for Spanish translations in order to help its expansion efforts in Mexico. Joe mentioned briefly that he knew the quality of our work, and that he would recommend us without hesitation. Jane responded to both Joe and to us saying she would be interested in meeting with us. She suggested we visit her booth at the upcoming gaming expo the following week.

❧ Be prepared. We had pre-arranged a meeting with Jane at a convenient time for her, and we secured a tradeshow pass through Joe, whose company was also exhibiting at the expo. We had researched Jane's company, and she had researched ours, too. "The company" was very interested in our services, and Jane assured us she would get back to us with projects. We briefly discussed our rates, which were acceptable to Jane. Five months later, "the company" sent us its first project and it is now a repeat customer.

❧ Show your appreciation. A few weeks later, we took Joe to lunch as a small thank-you for his efforts. We wanted him to know that we do not take introductions for granted, and that we were grateful to him for having established the business connection for us. We also sent a thank-you note to Jane for her interest in our services immediately after the tradeshow.

As you can see, establishing business relationships with direct customers is a big task, but it gets easier and more efficient with time. We have no doubt that every single one of us, regardless of how introverted we are, can find direct customers and develop solid working relationships with them.

There is no finish line

Both the good and the bad thing about direct customer acquisition is that you are never truly done. You will not really reach a point at which you can relax, count your blessings, and decide that you have enough customers. You should not do that because things change: your contact might leave the company, the company might go under, etc. You have to constantly refresh your pool of clients, and this is a never-ending project. You can always go to one more mixer, present at one more conference, or give one more interview. Do not let this discourage you. Quite the contrary: there are more possibilities than any of us could imagine.

CHAPTER 6

೪

PRICING

Do pricing theories and economics sound tedious to you? The nitty-gritty details of economic theories, including pricing calculations, charts, and calculus-based formulas can be quite overwhelming. Let us assure you that in this section, we will keep it basic and solely discuss real-life pricing as it applies to you. The only math you will need is what is needed to balance your checkbook, add up your invoices for your accounts receivable, etc. – and that is what calculators, spreadsheets, and specialized software are for.

Supply and demand

If you only remember one thing from this chapter, it should be that, at its most basic, price is determined by the intersection of supply and demand. Here is a simple example. U.S. consumers love to buy avocados to make guacamole. Recently, we have noticed that the price of an avocado is averaging around $1.50 a piece as opposed to roughly $0.80 a piece last year. This is a classic example of supply and demand. It is possible that the supply of avocados produced has decreased. There could be many causes for this, including labor disputes, an increase in the price of fertilizer needed to grow the plants, or natural causes such as a draught or a pest infestation. If demand stays the same, but the supply decreases, the prices will go up, as there are more people who want to buy avocados than there are avocados available. It is also possible that the demand for avocados has increased. Causes for increased demand could include seasonal spikes in demand surrounding such uniquely American celebrations as the Super Bowl and Cinco de Mayo.

This example is simply meant to illustrate the basic law of supply and demand. The markets for translation and interpretation are far more complicated. Prices will vary between language pairs and depend on the complexity of the source text or mode of interpretation, project turnaround time, and many other factors. That said, the key to setting your prices is understanding the value of your services to the client, and differentiating yourself from the competition. Stated another way, you must understand what kind of avocados you are supplying. Are they jumbo organic gourmet avocados for which you have little competition and for which there is high demand? If so, you can charge a premium. If on the other hand, you are supplying small tasteless avocados, then you are simply supplying an easily exchangeable commodity, and must accept what the buyer is willing to pay. What you should strive to do is position yourself as providing a superior service, which is in short supply and will result in increased demand. For more information on how to differentiate your services, please read the marketing chapter.

A note on rates

While we will be addressing general strategies and ideas about pricing, we will not be able to provide information about how much you should charge for your specific translation or interpretation services. Prices differ significantly between languages, specializations, years of experience, country, and much more. The decision on how much to charge for your services is complex and personal. Legislation on pricing varies significantly between countries, with some countries' associations issuing price recommendations, while other associations are legally prohibited from doing so. In order to comply with the rules and regulations in your country, please consult your national association of translators and interpreters.

Commodities

Commodities are mainly physical products, such as grains, food, and metals that are easily interchangeable with other products of the same type. They are traded on commodities markets around the world based on price, which is subject to supply and demand. For our purposes, we will say that non-differentiated avocados could also be seen as a commodity. To the purchaser, commodities are indistinguishable from other products in the same class, as they are not differentiated. This means that they only characteristic that is relevant to the buyer is the price of the product, which makes the product a commodity. You want to prevent positioning your services as a commodity, because then you will have to compete on price, and the high quality of your product, or your special expertise in a certain area, or your inside knowledge of a specific industry will not be relevant to the buyer. This means that you have wasted a significant amount of time and effort (education, experience, professional development) and are in a vulnerable position in terms of pricing. Think about it this way: you want to provide a service that is highly valued for its high quality rather than its cheap price.

For instance, the German carmaker BMW certainly does not compete on price. Quite the contrary: the prices are very high, but the world is largely in agreement that the company's cars are worth the price tag because they are well-made luxury cars. The company's defining characteristic is quality, not price. BMW has perfected the art of differentiating its products by creating the ultimate luxury vehicle. Potential buyers understand that high quality comes at a price, and know that a BMW costs more than a basic Toyota. You should try to get to that same spot with your customers: make them understand and appreciate your services for their top-notch quality rather than their price. You prevent your services from becoming commodities by differentiating yourself from the competition.

If your customers view your service as a commodity, they will not value anything else that you excel at and will judge your services solely on your price, typically always looking for the cheapest one. In our industry, this means that someone with a graduate degree in translation or interpretation from a top-notch university will be competing with someone who speaks neither the source nor the target language and works with Babelfish. Of course, the latter's services will be cheaper. However, as a professional linguist, you do not want to be thrown into a group where you have to compete with non-professionals solely based on price. By doing that, in the long run, you are sending the customer the message that your services can be purchased at rock-bottom prices. You are devaluating your services as a language professional, and telling customers that it is perfectly fine to choose the vendor with the lowest price. It is not. What should matter in our industry is the quality, not the price. By not competing on price, you will actually help elevate our industry and help it be taken more seriously as a professional service.

Why should I not compete on price?

Competing on price is bad because there will always be someone who will provide services cheaper than you. This means that as long as we are competing on price, there will be a competitor in the marketplace who is willing to undercut your prices. This competitor might not live on the same continent, so his/her financial situation might be completely different in terms of cost of living, expenses, etc. By competing solely on price, you are voluntarily turning yourself into a commodity. Companies of all sizes typically go to all kinds of trouble to avoid becoming a commodity, and you should do the same.

On a small business level, the following will happen to you if you compete on price:

No matter what your price, you will be undercut. We have seen rates as low as a few cents per word for major European languages. Granted, those translations are frequently not done by professionals. As serious linguists, we know that the quality of those translations is usually pretty low. Unfortunately, many customers do not know that. We are all responsible for informing customers that there tends to be a direct correlation between quality and price.

By advertising that your rates are low, customers will constantly ask you for discounts. Where do you draw the line? When is it cheap enough? How can you ensure that you make a living?

By competing on price, the following happens to our industry:

Potential customers are unable to distinguish between providers based on quality and will, because it is human nature, seek out the lowest price.

Barriers to entry into the business are already quite low, meaning that there is no exam you need to pass or other significant obstacle preventing competitors from entering the market. As the price drops and as long as demand exists, individuals who do not have solid translation qualifications will want to get into the market.

This means that the quality of the translation services provided will decrease and our entire industry will suffer, because quality cannot be guaranteed.

The fundamental problem in our industry is that the customer is likely to find a language services professional who will work for a very low price (for a variety of reasons). Ideally, linguists around the world, regardless of specialization, language combination, and country of residence, would agree that translation and interpretatation are professional services, and that they should be priced accordingly. It is possible that we might help reverse the trend towards low rates and position ourselves as providers of highly differentiated services who command fair and professional rates. Unfortunately, there will always be competitors who do not think about the impact that long-term price undercutting has on our industry and its reputation.

Pricing alternatives

It is quite possible that your client thinks that your prices are too high. When you feel downward pressure on prices, you should try to offer your clients some alternatives. We generally advise against directly negotiating the per unit price, but that is difficult to do. Here are a few things you could offer to do without changing your per word (or per line, or per hour) rate, thus signaling to your potential client that you are accommodating and want to work with them to reach a reasonable pricing agreement.

    Offer a discount on a rush fee. Many linguists charge a rush fee, and so should you. The definition of rush fee is up to you. It could be defined as any job that is assigned on a Friday to be turned in on a Monday (resulting in weekend work), 24-hour turnaround, 48-hour turnaround, etc. Sometimes, upon realizing that our rates are not within our potential customer's range, which is mostly the case with projects that include the rush fee, we will signal our willingness to work with the client by offering a small discount (say 10%) on the rush fee. Send a new, updated quote with the discount clearly highlighted.

    Offer a discount on a PDF surcharge. An additional fee to work on PDFs is routinely charged by many translators, as it is fairly difficult to work in these types of documents, sometimes even with specialized conversion software such as ABBYY Fine Reader. If your client appears to be sensitive to price, you could offer a discount on the PDF surcharge (again, around 10%) and phrase it along the lines of: "As a one-time customer courtesy to you, we would like to offer you a 10% discount on our PDF surcharge. We hope this will help you with your budget a bit. We look forward to hearing from you."

    Offer to throw in a bonus. You could offer something that is a soft cost to you. For instance, you could suggest turning the document in a day earlier than requested if the client seems to be rushed ("as a courtesy to you") or offer a free review of their source document if it sounds like this is something the client would be interested in.

    In extreme cases, offer to apply the non-profit price. While we are careful with discounts, we do offer special rates to non-profit organizations. We serve on the board of several associations of that kind, so we know that funds are always tight. It is just another way for us to give back to the community. If we really want to work with a customer whose business is geared towards serving the greater good, even if it is not a non-profit, we will offer them half the non-profit discount as a signal of our goodwill. However, this is a last resort, and we do not like to do it often.

✒ Apply an expired offer if you must. We send out notices once or twice a year about special offers that we offer on a select number of occasions. For instance, we offered a holiday special for all new clients during the month of December. In January, a potential client called and was looking for a less expensive quote than the one we had provided. We offered to honor the holiday special, even though it had expired, and applied that to the quote (the per-word rate remained unchanged). Our customer was happy and accepted the price quote.

Figuring out your ideal price can be complex, and in price negotiations, nothing is black or white. Give yourself some room to maneuver and show your potential customer that you are trying to work with them. For more tips on this process, please refer to the negotiating chapter.

The seller sets the price

For many linguists, pricing is a touchy subject that they do not want to discuss in detail, because it seems too – well, business-like. That is a mistake – we are all businesses, so unless you plan on running a non-profit, price is one of the most fundamental things you need to focus on. Even if you have been trained that price is something for the business folks and that the humanities people like yourself should focus on the finer aspect of languages, you need to re-think that strategy. Start treating price discussions and negotiations as an integral part of your business. It might not be your favorite part of the businesses, but you are most likely the only one who can and will do it. With time, you might grow to love pricing strategies, because you will be able to see instant rewards.

In general, a modern economy works because the seller sets the price, not the buyer. Think about this for a second. How many times have you had customers approach you and say "We pay X" or "Our rates are Y"? To this, you could say: "Thank you very much for this information. My rates are Z." As the seller, you set the rate. Setting your own price is not only paramount to getting what you want out of your business – in terms of professional, financial, and personal success – but is also a critical corner point in negotiating. If you do not set your own price, you are sending the message that you must be a weak negotiating partner. Price setting is an art and not a science, and there are exceptions to the rule. For instance, if a client comes to you with a very large project requesting a lower rate than you usually charge, you might consider it if the project is highly lucrative overall. In that case, the buyer would indeed be setting the price, and it is still up to you whether you agree to it or not. The larger the seller's company, the more likely they are to do price setting. For instance, many large companies will buy consulting and accounting services for all their subsidiaries from the same vendors. In return for that significant amount of business, the client will oftentimes state that they would like to pay a certain amount of money.

Pricing case study: the massage therapist

Let us give you an example of a real-life situation with pricing and price-setting. Earlier this year, we decided it was time to schedule occasional massages for our computer-related maladies, including tight shoulders and stiff necks. Judy found a massage therapist who came highly recommended and who works at a local spa, but who also does massages at clients' home and uses an advanced therapy for very tight muscles. Judy called him, talked to him, and was informed that his rate was $45 for 60 minutes. He never mentioned a tip, but Judy decided to include at least $10 for a tip every session. After ten sessions, the massage therapist, Jason, decided that he would give Judy a free massage because of her repeat business. Judy was delighted and has booked regular massages with Jason ever since.

The lesson behind this story is that Jason, the massage therapist, is the seller. Thus, he sets the price. As the buyer, you have two choices: you either accept the price, or you do not and go somewhere else. These are the only two choices available to you, unless you live in a country where bargaining is the cultural norm. Judy did not try to argue with Jason because she respects his profession and the prices he demands for his services. If she had been buying pottery at a Mexican outdoor market, of course she would have bargained. However, bargaining for professional services is simply not done nor is it acceptable in most countries.

Let us analyze the previous scenario if Judy had pretended that she, the buyer, set the price in her conversation with Jason. Surely this will sound familiar to you from conversations you have had with existing and potential clients.

Judy: "So I hear that you are a wonderful massage therapist. My friend Natasha recommended you very highly. Tell me more about your services."

Jason: "Thanks for calling. Yes, Natasha is a long-time client of mine, and I am thankful for her recommendation. I have been a licensed massage therapist for more than 20 years and have worked with Olympic athletes and performers in local shows here in Las Vegas. I specialize in helping hard-working entrepreneurs relax and loosen their muscles."

Judy: "That is wonderful; it is precisely what I need! How much are your sessions?"

Jason (very friendly): "I am glad you think so. My fee is $45 an hour, and I will come to your house with all my equipment whenever is convenient for you."

Judy (sure of herself): "OK. I am sure you can do better than that, right?"

Jason (slightly confused): "I am not sure I understand what you mean. My hours are quite flexible and I can also come to your office if you would like."

Judy (with conviction): "Well, I am talking about the price. I am sure we can agree on a better price. How about $30 per session?"

Jason (softly): "Ah, I see. No, unfortunately, the rate is fixed at $45. You will find that it is worth every penny and that your productivity will increase once your muscles are more relaxed and your pain is gone."

Judy (slightly annoyed): "Oh, but surely you can give me a special deal? After all, I will be coming to see you for many years. I will also recommend you to my friends if I like you. Let us settle on $35 per session. That is my final offer."

Jason (more confused now): "I appreciate your intention of becoming a repeat customer. Unfortunately, the rates are the same for everyone."

Judy (stubborn): "Well, call me back when you can offer me a decent price. This is not going to cut it."

Jason deletes Judy's phone number from his cell phone and hopes he never hears from her again.

Does a conversation along these lines ring a bell? Has it happened to you that you have to constantly justify your prices during a conversation with a potential client? This example is meant to illustrate that haggling usually does not work for products (unless they are defective or the buyer has significant purchasing power) or services sold in formal business environments (read: not outdoor markets). Please see our chapter on negotiating to learn more about how to deal with difficult situations.

Do not complain about low prices

It is certainly very disappointing when, as a professional linguist, you are offered low rates for the highly specialized and challenging work you do. However, this is a free economy, and you are under no obligation to accept prices you do not want to work for. After all, you work for yourself and ultimately do not have an obligation toward anyone else. Remember: you are the boss, but also the employee. So, if you think that you are not being compensated fairly for your services, there are two things you can do:

- Do nothing and complain to all of your friends and colleagues about it, many of whom might be in the same boat.

- Do something about it.

Are you ready to do something about it? Here are some ideas that might help you raise your prices, raise your self esteem, and will allow you to make a good living.

- Develop a new pricing strategy that will allow you to live according to your needs and make the profit you would like to make.

- Approach your existing clients with your new prices.

- Communicate your prices early in the process.

- If your old clients are reluctant to pay your newer, higher prices, which is likely, try to transition away from them and slowly find and cultivate a new customer base that is less price-sensitive.

- Develop a pricing sheet and put it on your website.

- Set the expectation that your prices are firm, and that no haggling is allowed.

Yearly price adjustments for inflation

This is an important issue, and one that has been debated quite a bit in the translation and interpretation world. Many linguists feel very strongly about this topic, whether they are for adjustments or against them, and both positions are more than valid. Whether you adjust your prices for inflation or not is ultimately a personal decision and will depend strongly on your situation, your language combination, the country you live in, and on a variety of other factors. It is also important that you have a look at the global economy and inflation rates overall, especially in your main country of business, which might not be the same as the country in which you reside. We recommend thinking about adjusting your prices for inflation on a yearly basis. If you have heard about price adjustments, but you cannot remember the last time you adjusted your rates, you should read on. Inflation is the rise in general price levels over time, and it results in decreasing purchasing power. That means, in a nutshell, that we will not be able to buy the same products for the same prices at some point in the future. Rather, they will become more expensive over time.

Why should I adjust my rates for inflation?

Without going too deep into this somewhat complicated field, we will make it simple and say that pretty much everything in the marketplace gets more expensive over time. This includes food staples, housing, insurance, etc. This means that, if your salary stayed the same, you would have less purchasing power in year two than you had in year one. This is called inflation. Historically, inflation in the U.S. has run between 3% and 5% in the last few years. This number is significantly higher in other countries, especially less industrialized nations, where inflation can skyrocket. To compensate employees for the increase in the cost of goods in the marketplace and to ensure that their purchasing power stays the same, many employers in the U.S. offer what are called yearly salary adjustments. They are not considered (nor are they) raises. Before you become alarmed and think that your customers might be taken aback by these kinds of adjustments, remember that you are dealing with customers on a business-to-business basis. This means that your customers have, more than likely, also adjusted their rates to keep up with inflation. As an entrepreneur in our industry, you have to pass the adjustment for inflation on to your customers. If you do not adjust your prices for inflation for many years, your purchasing power will decrease significantly because of compound inflation, which is the same principle as for compound interest. In short, over time, inflation will severely impact your standard of living if you do not periodically adjust your prices for inflation.

How to adjust your prices for inflation

Remember that adjusting your prices is only possible if you have distinguished your services from your competition. When you do adjust your prices for inflation, you should consider doing it yearly at the same time each year. You should either post your prices on your website or have them readily available for customers and potential customers to view. In the U.S., check the Bureau of Labor Statistics for the most up-to-date inflation data: http://www.bls.gov/cpi/.

Even though the per-unit (line, hour, word) price adjustment will be very small, you should probably communicate your adjustment to your clients, especially if you are doing it for the first time. There are several options for doing this:

&. Make an asterisk next to your prices on your online rate sheet and add "Prices have been adjusted for inflation as of date X."

&. If you feel more comfortable letting your existing customers know via e-mail, go ahead and do so. Keep it brief and simply state that you are sending a new rate sheet for their information with the rates for the upcoming year. Blind copy yourself on this e-mail so you have documentation should a problem arise.

Another option is to add a sentence to any new invoice that you are issuing in the new year. It could simply say: "Please note that our rates have been adjusted for inflation as of date X."

Please remember that these strategies apply to direct clients. We have no experience working with translation agencies, but we have heard that many are quite reluctant to adjust freelance translators' or interpreters' rates for inflation, even though the agencies themselves do adjust their rates for inflation with their clients. Start thinking like an entrepreneur and bring up this issue. Any business will understand this basic fact of the marketplace: prices go up and rates need to be adjusted accordingly.

Non-negotiable prices

Stating anywhere in your marketing materials or on your website that your prices are negotiable is not a good business decision. Intuitively, every buyer (and every seller) knows that prices can be negotiable at some point. However, this does not mean you should be advertising this. You should not make it appear as if you were completely open to negotiating your prices. Again, you are the seller, so you need to act like the professional business that you are and set a specific price. If potential customers want to negotiate with you, you certainly cannot stop them. What you can control is your side of the negotiation. For more information on negotiating, please read the next chapter.

http://mox.ingenierotraductor.com

© 2009 AMR - Based on an idea by G. Chamard

CHAPTER 7

&.

NEGOTIATING

The art of negotiating

Negotiating is something you do constantly in your everyday life, not just when it comes to pricing a particular translation or interpretation project. You negotiate with your mechanic about when you can have your car back, with your friends about where to meet for happy hour, with your children about their bedtime, and with your other half about who does the dishes. These are negotiations on all kinds of different levels, but in all of them, you are one of the parties trying to reach agreement on a particular issue. That agreement should ideally be acceptable to both parties.

Negotiating is one of the most challenging aspects of running a business, especially if you are the only person working for your business. This means that you will not able to hand the negotiation process over to someone who is more skilled at it than you, like you might in a larger company. Basically, negotiating is a tug-of-war between what you, the seller, and your customer, the buyer, want. Rarely will you both want the same thing. As a customer, you would naturally want to obtain the lowest price for whatever product or service you want to purchase, so you cannot blame your customers for trying to negotiate. On the other hand, as a professional, you probably rarely negotiate price with fellow professionals – lawyers, doctors, accountants – yet for some reason, customers are constantly trying to negotiate with linguists as if they were at a Moroccan spice market. The solution to this problem is to be firm on price and to educate your clients that professional language services cannot be negotiated on price. To read more pricing strategies, please have a closer look at the pricing chapter. Last year, we discovered a fantastic, highly professional video about the vendor-client relationship in the real world and its challenges when it comes to price negotiation. It beautifully illustrates some of the problems we face as entrepreneurs when negotiating with clients. You can view the video at http://tinyurl.com/rxvuxc.

The basics of negotiating

Know your bottom line. You might remember from previous chapters that we generally advise you not to negotiate on price. However, the business world is not all black and white, and there are some gray areas. This means that you might have to negotiate on price occasionally, but in general, try to stay away from it. Knowing your bottom line includes being firm on the parameters that you will not compromise on. They could be delivery time and date or the area of specialization. For instance, if you know that it is not possible for you to deliver 4,000 words by tomorrow, say so firmly. Do not let the other party pressure you into something you are not willing to compromise on. You should, however, include in your negotiation certain tokens – that is, items that are not that important to you that you can use for negotiating. For instance, you could say that you would like documents to be delivered in a specific format, even if you do not feel very strongly about it. Then, if the negotiation gets down to the nitty-gritty, you could consider saying: "I will be happy to work with you and, as a courtesy to you; I will accept your files in a format that I do not typically accept." This way, your negotiating partner will feel that he or she has gained something, even if it is something that is not that relevant to you. Give yourself some room to maneuver. A good strategy to know which things you are willing to compromise on and which you do not is to write them down on a simple piece of paper. Regardless of whether the conversation is taking place via telephone, e-mail or in person, you should know what to stick with.

🐾 **Be prepared.** This is true and very important of every business conversation, not only negotiations. Do your research. The more you know about your negotiating partner and his or her company, the better. Invest a little bit of time in your potential business partner by reading press releases and current company data. You never know what you might discover. Perhaps you will find out that the company has just pulled out of the international market or that they are planning a major expansion into a market that might be very lucrative for you. Also, do a brief online search on your negotiating partner. You might learn, for instance, that you have several business partners and former or current colleagues in common. Whatever you find out, use it to set a cordial negotiating tone by pointing out what you have in common and creating a comfortable atmosphere for your conversation.

It is not a war. Have you observed real-life lawyers at depositions and in court? Unless you watch a lot of lawyers on TV, you know that most of their interactions are quite cordial and that they will engage in friendly banter and conversation. The same is true for business negotiations. We are all just doing our jobs and trying to do the best we can for ourselves and our company, so it is not a war, but rather just a business conversation. Although some people can become quite aggressive during negotiations, think of it as analogous to a sporting competition. You will both give everything you have on the field of play, but once you are done, you shake your opponent's hand. Negotiating is similar to that.

It is not personal. We are constantly working on perfecting the art of not taking things personally. It certainly feels personal when you negotiate and the other party is trying to get you to agree to terms that might not work for you. Think of it the way your negotiating partner, your potential customer, might look at it. Any buyer would want to get the best price and the best deal from all vendors. No one is alleging that your services are not good or that they are not worth what you are asking. People simply want a better deal. Some business professionals, as a matter of principle, do not accept the first offer that comes across their desk. They like the negotiating process and want to hone their skills, too. In addition, your negotiating partner might just be trying to proof to her boss that she can lead successful price negotiations with vendors. Perhaps her raise depends on negotiating you down to a specific amount? You never know what the other person's agenda is, but rest assured that they have nothing against you personally, nor are they making a statement about your competency.

Practice. Consider reading a book on negotiating if you have the time and the interest to learn more about this process. Alternatively, you can further your skills by practicing, ideally in real-life situations. If you feel that you do not have the chance to practice much in actual business situations, practice your skills in mock situations with friends or colleagues. Negotiating in person is more challenging than negotiating over the phone, so practice both. Practicing might be difficult and time-consuming, but you will get better, and you will be more relaxed and feel more empowered during the actual negotiations. The more empowered you feel, the better you will negotiate. You may also notice that many clients will either accept your price or will try to negotiate via e-mail. For that purpose, consider creating templates with standard text that you can use over and over again.

Silence. This famous negotiating trick is quite effective. If your negotiating partner calls you and says: "The price that you quoted is completely unrealistic, I really cannot pay you that; it is ridiculous," you respond by saying nothing; by keeping quiet. It will be uncomfortable, but try not to say anything for a few seconds. These seconds will seem like an hour, but the silence might be effective in that it will make your negotiating partner uncomfortable as well. Silence is very awkward for the vast majority of people, and we tend to avoid it as much as possible. Try this strategy and see what happens. In our experience, the response has been: "Well, okay, I guess the price is not so bad after all." It is quite astonishing what a few seconds of silence can do for you.

Ignore the need to justify yourself. This is also a tough skill to master. But by the time your potential client is ready to negotiate with you, he or she should already have all sorts of information about you: a company presentation, a link to your website, a professional quote, perhaps a short bio, etc. It should already be abundantly clear to your potential customer why your services are priced the way they are. Hence, now is not the time to say: "My services cost XYZ because I have XYZ years' experience in the translation industry; I have worked on high-profile projects, etc." Your negotiating partner already has all this information. So he or she wants to negotiate in spite of knowing your qualifications. Do not feel like you need to justify yourself and stand by your quote as much as possible.

Walk away. Sometimes a negotiation will end without an agreement, meaning you will not get any business, which is an acceptable outcome. Do not look at it as failure. Rather, look at it as a conscious decision not to enter into a business relationship because you decided that it was not a good deal for you. This is one of the many advantages of running your own business: you can choose who you work with. Similarly, the other side might decide that they do not want to work with you. At all times, be polite, thank the other person for their time, analyze what you could possibly learn from this interaction, and move on.

You get what you negotiate. Unfortunately, there is no divine justice in negotiating and you will not be paid what you think you are worth simply because you have a great reputation and are an outstanding linguist. You will not necessarily get paid what you are worth, but you will get paid what you negotiate. Hence, you need to negotiate smartly. If you are not getting what you are worth or what you want, analyze the market, see if your price range is reasonable, and if it is: practice, practice, practice.

Advanced negotiating tips

🐾 You are not running for class president. Be prepared that some of your negotiating strategies will not make you universally popular at all times, and that is fine. You are trying to get business done and not trying to win popularity contest.

🐾 **Learn to deal with difficult people.** Just like you, the person you are negotiating with will also try to learn about negotiation and improve his or her skills. Some individuals might use intimidation techniques, they might yell, or they might try to play mental tricks on you. Be prepared for these behaviors and maintain a cool head.

🐾 **Keep your composure.** The worst thing you can do during a negotiation is to lose your professional demeanor. Even when your negotiation partner is not playing fair, is raising her voice, and is completely unreasonable, you should remain calm and professional.

🐾 **International negotiation.** Be aware that certain cultures are more direct than others when negotiating. In addition, there are vast differences in the way people from different cultures communicate, and therefore, negotiate. Before you go into a meeting or negotiation with someone from a cultural background that you are not very familiar with, do some research. It is respectful and courteous to be informed, and it might also give you a negotiating edge, because you will have developed a little bit of insight into the other person's behaviors.

🐾 **Watch body language.** Once you have some practice negotiating, you will realize that people might say one thing, but that their body language might tell a different story. Learn to pay attention to the non-verbal cues, such as closed positions, signaling resistance (crossed legs and arms), facial expressions and eyes, and even torso positioning.

🐾 **Listen without prejudice.** Most of us think we are fairly good listeners. But have you caught yourself listening only halfheartedly as you mentally prepare your own response? Have you noticed that you only really listen to the information that you could use? Try moving away from that and truly listen to what the other person has to say. Read between the lines and listen, listen, listen. If you have not had time to formulate your response when the other person has finished talking, take a few seconds to collect your thoughts.

Show empathy. Contrary to popular belief, you do not have to be a hard-headed bully to be a good negotiator. Quite the opposite: many outstanding negotiators have the ability to really understand what the other party needs or wants. Start by acknowledging what the other party wants. Respect the fact that negotiating comes down to humans trying to make compromises, and that empathy can be a crucial factor in a successful negotiation. No one will compromise with you if you cannot show empathy. While you do not have to agree with what others are saying, you can indeed acknowledge their message or feelings. If empathy is not your forte, focus on putting yourself in the other person's shoes and take it from there.

Identify your weaknesses and work on them. While most great negotiators share certain traits – patience, flexibility, respect for others, empathy, integrity, sense of humor, etc. – no one is born a master negotiator. Take the time to identify the areas that you can improve. Practice with a colleague or a loved one, in front of a pet or simply a mirror. If you can, record yourself either on audio or video during a mock negotiation. Ask for feedback. It might feel silly, but you will get more comfortable as you practice in no-risk situations.

http://mox.ingenierotraductor.com

© 2009 Alejandro Moreno-Ramos

CHAPTER 8

ঌ

PROFESSIONAL DEVELOPMENT

Steven Covey, the well-known author of management books, frequently mentions that all professionals need to "sharpen their saw." This means that one needs to constantly keep on learning and expanding one's knowledge. As linguists, we already learn a tremendous amount of information on a daily basis, but we also need to learn in a structured environment with other professionals at conferences and workshops. They are a great opportunity to expand your knowledge, and also give you the chance to meet and network with fellow linguists, translation buyers, and others in our business.

However, in these tough economic times, it is tempting to forego professional development. Traditionally, more individuals attend college or take professional courses during challenging economic times. If you have some dry spells in terms of work, do not let it frustrate you. Rather, use some of the downtime to improve what you already know, to deepen your knowledge in a specific area, or to expand into other specializations. In addition, the learning you do does not have to be directly related to translation or interpretation. There are many other skills you could learn or improve, such as business-related skills (accounting, taxation for small businesses), management skills (time management), or entrepreneurial skills such as growing your business.

Conference checklist

How often you should attend a professional development event is a very individual decision. As a general rule, we suggest attending a workshop, seminar or conference a few times a year, time and budget permitting. Most countries' national translation and interpretation organizations offer regular conferences, sometimes several every year. In addition, there are many smaller organizations, such as regional and state chapters, that also put on workshops, lectures, and events. If you hold a translation certification, be sure to inquire how many hours of professional development credits you must obtain to keep your certification current. Attending a conference or workshop will most likely leave you invigorated, refreshed, and with lots of new knowledge. In addition, in a profession that is as solitary as ours, going out and spending several days with likeminded professionals is a real treat and contributes to our emotional well-being. If you can afford to go to several events and workshops a year, that is fantastic. Do not be deterred by the cost of going to conferences. You could also substitute a conference with a series of webinars (seminars held via the web), which are oftentimes free and are becoming more and more popular. You will not have the chance to meet colleagues physically, but you can at least participate in workshops even if your budget is quite strained.

Here is a short planning checklist for your in-person professional development activities:

Where will the event be held, geographically? Is it close enough for you to drive to? This will make a difference in terms of financial planning. Being able to drive to the event will substantially decrease your expenses and might make it more feasible for you to attend.

Is it in a different time zone? If it is, you need to plan that into your schedule for the week of the conference. If you live on the American West Coast and you are going to a conference in say, Chicago, you will need an entire day for travel each way, between flights and the time difference. If you are coming from another country, the time difference is even more substantial and you should not underestimate the time it will take you to get acclimated. Plan accordingly and inform your customers how long you will be gone, including travel time.

Book early to get the early bird specials. Save money by booking everything as early as you can, including your flights. Sign up for your favorite airline's e-mail list, which will ensure you get the best deals delivered to your mailbox. When looking for a both a flight and a hotel, have a look at the packages offered by major airlines and travel websites. Unless the hotel offers a low conference special, packages can usually save quite a bit of money.

How expensive is the conference city in terms of lodging and food? Pocatello, Idaho is cheaper than New York City. Do some online research to see what the average prices for hotels and restaurants are. Do not forget that in some cities, mainly big convention cities like Las Vegas and Orlando, hotel prices tend to fluctuate depending on whether there is a big convention in town. That means that to get an exact price for the time you are thinking about going, you will need to search for the specific date of the conference. Most major hotel chains will let you make free online reservations. Make a note in your calendar to cancel the reservation should you change your mind. In general, you can cancel without penalty between 24 -72 hours prior to your arrival day. Many large conferences that are held in major hotels negotiate special hotel rates for their attendees. These are called "room blocks," and usually feature a limited number of rooms. They typically sell out well in advance of the conference, at which point the price for rooms will go to the hotel's regular rate. This rate can be up to double of the rate that has been negotiated for the room block. Reserve as far ahead of time as you can, even if you are not 100% sure you will be attending yet or if you are still shopping around for better deals. However, if you choose to not use the room you reserved at the conference hotel, be nice to your colleagues and contact them to see if someone else would like to take your reservation.

❧ **Do you have any close friends in the city you are going to?** If you do, is there anyone who could host you? If you want to minimize your expenses, this is the way to go, but be sure to consider the following:

❧ In case you need to work: is your friend's home equipped with wireless internet? If not, is there a computer you can use that is connected to the internet?

❧ How far is your friend's home from the conference venue?

❧ Will you be able to take public transportation, could you walk, or would you have to rent a car?

❧ When staying with a friend, be sure to bring a thoughtful gift for the hostess or host and take your friend(s) to dinner.

❧ **Decreasing the cost.** Do you have any miles or credit card points that you could use toward your trip? Before you plan your trip, look into some of the benefits of your credit cards or frequent flier cards. Take advantage of any travel deals or cash rewards that you might qualify for to decrease the cost of the trip. In addition, consider splitting the room costs with a colleague by looking for a roommate ahead of time. Many large conferences have blogs where users can post roommate requests.

ﬁ **Plan your schedule ahead of time.** Many conferences offer hundreds of sessions and classes, so in order to maximize your time, you should try to plan which sessions to attend ahead of time. This can easily be done by looking at the preliminary program that most conferences publish online. Some conferences even offer a software application that lets you create a customized electronic conference schedule. When you arrive at the event, check the finalized program to ensure there have been no changes to the schedule.

ﬁ **Plan your meetings and networking events ahead of time.** These events are also a great opportunity to meet with potential clients, colleagues, and new and old connections. In order to get the most out of your time, try to schedule lunches, coffee breaks, and dinners ahead of time Leave a few time slots open so you have some flexibility to spend time with other people you had not yet penciled into your schedule.

ﬁ **For those attending a large event for the first time,** it is normal to feel intimidated and overwhelmed, especially if you do not know any fellow linguists or are unable to connect with those you already know. Many conferences, such as the American Translators Association, help newcomers by inviting them to the first-time attendees' orientation session on the first day of the conference. This session, which we encourage you to attend, will tell you more about the event and help you sort through the hundreds of choices you have. You will also receive great tips on how to get the most out of your days at the conference. In addition, if you would like, you can attach a "first-time attendee" flag to your name badge. It might seem awkward at first, but people will actually come up to you, introduce themselves, show you around and ask you how they can make your experience better. More often than not, you will end up with a new friend, acquaintance, or a business contact, and you might have someone to join you for lunch. If you are traveling by yourself and staying in the conference hotel, resist the urge to head to your room when you have a break between sessions. It is tempting to forego networking, but since you allocate a limited time each year to conferences and networking, you should try to get the most out of it. As long as there are events, networking sessions, and happy hours taking place in the hotel, you should try to attend. While it is no fun walking into an event of any type by yourself, you should do it anyway. As introverted as many linguists say they are, it is amazing how friendly and outgoing they are at conferences. Resist the temptation of bringing a spouse, as that will significantly cut down on your networking opportunities.

Send an "upcoming vacation" alert two weeks before your departure. Let clients, business partners and colleagues know ahead of time when you will be gone so they can plan accordingly. Send out a quick e-mail two weeks before you go. It is fine to send out a mass e-mail, but be sure to blind-copy everyone so recipients cannot see each others' e-mail addresses. Clearly state when you will be out of the office. If there is a business partner or colleague who will be available while you are away, indicate that in your message.

Program an out-of-office message and test it before you go. Programming an out-of-office message, which recipients will receive as an automatic reply when they e-mail you, is very important so your contacts and potential customers know you are away and are not simply failing to respond. The precise way of programming an out-of-office message depends on your e-mail server, but it is usually quite straightforward. After you activate it, send yourself a test message from another account to verify that you will actually receive a correct out-of-office message (and that it does not have old dates in it).

Be reachable for your customers, even when you are away. In today's global 24/7 business world, it is very possible that some of your customers expect you to be available all the time. While this might or might not be realistic and/or reasonable, you should make an effort to be reachable. This does not mean that you have to run out and get a smart phone or have your cell phone on vibrate while you are attending educational sessions. Just ensure that your customers know where to reach you. Check your messages and e-mails a few times a day and call back if you can. Busy conventions and conferences are usually not the ideal venue to return business phone calls, but find as quiet a spot as you can. Your customer should already know that you are at a conference furthering your skills, so if he or she hears noise in the background, it is the conference noise that is to be expected.

Take an hour or two (or three, or four) to do something fun during the conference. Hopefully, the conference will take place in a city that you have yet to visit, which makes for a great sightseeing opportunity. This should not interfere with the work you are here to do – that is, the sessions that you want to attend, the networking you want to do – but you can always find a bit of time to see the sights as well. You could take this as an opportunity to invite a friend or colleague along and take your relationship from virtual to real-life. In our global business, we do not have that many opportunities to spend time together and get to know one another on a personal, non-virtual level, so spend some extra time with one of your favorite colleagues (or soon-to-be favorite colleagues).

🕭 **Meet up with bloggers.** If you are an active translation blogger and/or use Twitter as a marketing tool, consider organizing or attending a bloggers' lunch or an informal get-together at a conference. There have been several great bloggers' lunches at the annual American Translators Association's conference, where everyone connected and talked about their blogging experience.

🕭 **Travel smarts.** When sharing meals with colleagues, get a separate check for your expenses, and do the same with receipts for taxi rides. Keep all receipts in an envelope to make your accounting a breeze at the end of the conference.

🕭 **Certificates of attendance and the art of marketing them.** Most conferences award certificates of attendance, which you should keep handy. If you are a certified translator or interpreter, check with the event organizers if the event qualifies for any continuing education points. You should also use your professional development activities as a marketing tool: let clients know that professional development is important to you and that you are continuously attending workshops, seminars, and classes while striving to improve your skills. Consider having a section on your website where you list the professional development events you have attended in the recent past.

Becoming a conference speaker

When we first started attending conferences, we were amazed how well-prepared the speakers were, and were impressed by their willingness to give advice, share what they know, and help others. It has been many years since we were at a conference with a first-time attendee flag attached to our badges, and now we have become speakers ourselves. Initially, we simply focused on learning and networking as much as possible, and were not thinking much about sharing what we knew with others. It took us a few years of going to conferences to identify subjects that were not being covered and that we are passionate about. For Dagmar, it is the new German ortography with all its changes, updates, and new rules, and for Judy, it is the "Entrepreneurial Linguist" series of workshops, which this book is partially based on. After we decided that it was time for us to share our insight with the rest of the languages community, things moved fairly quickly. We made a few contacts, did several presentations at smaller, regional chapters, and submitted abstracts to the larger conferences. For us, speaking at conferences is a tremendously rewarding experience, and we learn as much from the audience as they learn from us.

Is it for you?

It depends. If the thought of public speaking makes you break out in hives, then perhaps it is not for you. On the other hand, if you simply experience some minor nerves and perhaps a bit of stage fright, which are perfectly normal, then this might be something you can learn and enjoy. Like anything else, public speaking is a skill that can be acquired and practiced, and you will be amazed at how quickly you can become comfortable speaking in front of a group. Once you have given a few solid presentations, you will be reassured and hopefully look forward to sharing your expertise. A good resource for learning how to speak in public can be a local Toastmasters group, which is all about helping its members excel at public speaking. Find your local chapter at http://www.toastmasters.org/.

The financial bottom line

You will receive an honorarium plus expenses if you are the invited keynote speaker at a small number of select conferences, but these are few and far between. More often than not, you will have to pay your own way, and will even have to pay to attend the conference just like any other attendee. This is because most large conferences, such as the American Translator Association's annual conference, are run by non-profit organizations that try to keep costs really low for their members. They only have the funds to pay for a few select speakers. While you would ideally be compensated for your time and effort, look at these speaking engagements as opportunities to build your reputation and gain industry-wide recognition. You main goal should be to share what you know with fellow linguists around the world and to build your reputation. That being said, being a recognized leader and expert in your field is an excellent marketing tool. One of the first steps toward achieving that is to present at conferences and workshops. Once you are established enough as a speaker, people will remember you and your field of expertise. If a fellow linguist or a potential client is looking for a translator for a specific project, they are more likely to remember someone who is well-established; that may well be someone they have seen present at a conference. The names that conference attendees remember the most are usually those of people who have raised their profile by speaking at a workshop or conference.

How much work will it be?

The bad news is that it will be a lot of work, but you can do it at your own pace. Unless explicitly specified in the call for papers at the conference (mainly for academic conferences), you can present the same content at several events. We have several workshops that we present, and throughout the year we put at least 50 hours of work into each workshop. This includes time for developing the workshop, doing the research, tinkering with the layout, and dozens of hours of rehearsing and timing the presentation. You will gain confidence as you go along. It helps to present your workshop to a trusted partner or close friend to get honest feedback on the content of the workshop and on your presentation. For instance, when Judy first rehearsed her now popular "Entrepreneurial Linguist" workshop in front of Dagmar in Europe, Dagmar asked her to eliminate a few amusing anecdotes that work well for a U.S. audience, but that would not work that well in Europe. Judy learned some valuable lessons during that practice session. Try to rehearse your presentation in front of another languages professional, but regardless of the listener's profession, he or she is bound to have some good insight. Once you rehearse the workshop you have spent so long developing and writing, it often becomes clear that a few things are repetitive, or that some things need to be tweaked. Resist the temptation to go to a presentation without having rehearsed it thoroughly beforehand – that would be equivalent to handing in a translation without proofing it. Ask your listener to take notes on what you need to improve upon and review these notes carefully.

Finding your topic

Most linguists have an area that is of special interest to them, whether it is a specialization, a research interest, an academic field, or specific kinds of terminology. Put some thought into how your area of expertise could be interesting to a larger audience. Perhaps your area of translation specialization is renewable energies, a very timely and interesting topic. Perhaps you could discuss industry-specific legislation, terminology, business practices, or give some advice on how newcomers can get into the field. Should your preferred area of specialization be, say, candle making, that might be an interesting topic and a good, narrow, niche for your work life. However, it is not likely that this narrow subject matter would attract too much interest at conferences. Remember that your workshop first needs to be accepted into the conference program by the conference organizers. In your workshop proposal, you need to tell the conference committee why your presentation is a good fit for the event. Conferences usually receive significantly more applications for workshops than they can accept, sometimes up to five times as many, so to ensure you get a spot, your topic needs to be of interest to linguists who do not specialize in candle making. Thus, you could perhaps speak about the arts and crafts business and their needs for translation, present some case studies, and talk about the major companies who need the assistance of linguists to market their products around the world. You could also recommend applicable dictionaries and talk about life as a translator in this field.

Include some analysis of the market and any specific translation skills one needs to succeed in this particular area.

Are you a software guru or do you use a specific software tool that makes your life easier but that not many other people are familiar with? Perhaps you should propose a section on your favorite software tool, which is typically of great interest to both conference organizers and attendees. Pick a tool that is relevant to linguists across all fields, regardless of language combination or specialization. However, for conferences that are language- and specialization-specific, you can choose topics that are much more narrow and targeted. For instance, if you are a French to English legal translator and want to present some information on recent changes in French law, that might be of great interest to fellow translators in that language group. A friend of Judy's, Karen Tkaczyk, translates texts related to chemistry (French and Spanish into English). She frequently presents technical workshops that are not language-specific, and give translators excellent insight into the workings of the pharmaceutical, cosmetics and broader chemical industry. She also gives language-specific sessions at larger events where there is a big enough audience. Her workshops have been very popular with both seasoned professionals and people wanting to get into this specialization.

Applying to present at conferences

After you have established a reputation as an interesting speaker, conference organizers will most likely approach you. Until then, you will need to approach them. Our suggestion is to approach smaller regional conferences first so you can gain some confidence in front of smaller groups. When you make contact with chapters around the country or the world, keep in mind that they are all small non-profits run by volunteer board of directors whose members have to run their own translation or interpretation businesses and who do volunteer work in addition to a full-time workload. Thus, do not expect an immediate response, and be respectful of your colleagues' limited time. Most translation and interpretation organizations strive to provide as many professional development opportunities to their members as possible, and proposals are usually quite welcome. However, it is possible that the particular organization you have approached has given a similar workshop in the past or that it does not think it is a good fit for its members. Do not be discouraged and keep on trying. If your content is good and you are an interesting presenter who keeps the audience engaged, you will have the opportunity to give workshops. Sometimes it just takes time to get recognized as a speaker. When you approach organizations with your workshop, you should send the following:

❧ **Short e-mail.** Find out who the president, vice president and professional development director of the organization are. Then compose a short e-mail to them, introducing yourself as a fellow linguist and state that you would like to propose a professional development workshop for the organization. Mention that you are attaching an abstract and a short biography for the board's review.

❧ **Abstract.** This should be no longer than one page, and it should be in PDF format. Include a brief overview of your workshop and its content. If you have presented it before, include dates and organizations and a picture of you presenting if you have one. You can get creative here and include any other relevant information.

❧ **Short bio.** Your biography should also be no longer than one page, and it should also be in PDF format. Include your relevant work background, your translation and interpretation experience, and any other information you deem important. If you have a professional photo of yourself, include it.

Most large conferences will have websites with sections that detail the requirements you need to fulfill for submitting a presentation proposal, which you can oftentimes do through a convenient online portal. If that option is available, simply log on and follow the instructions.

Everyday professional development

Most of us either live or work in a country where our source or target language(s) are not the official languages, unless you happen to live in Canada, Switzerland or a few other countries. Thus, unless you are in the lucky position of dividing your time between the countries of your source and target language, you will need to keep your language skills current. Many linguists translate into their mother tongue, even if they have lived in the source language for many decades. In those cases, it is especially important to keep your language skills fresh. Language evolves and changes constantly: new words are added to the dictionary, others are no longer common usage, and foreign-language terms are becoming more and more acceptable. While it is daunting to have to keep your finger on the pulse of several languages, it is your job as a language professional to do so. Here are a few things you might consider doing on a daily basis to keep things fresh, especially for your target language, and in particular if you do not live in a country where the target language is spoken:

Daily reading. Spend some time every day reading the news and current events in the language you are trying to keep current. Sign up for the latest news via your favorite RSS reader, which compiles the news on your customized homepage. By reading we mean active reading, that is, actively acquiring new words, idioms, expressions, and vocabulary you might not be familiar with. Since most of your reading will likely be done online, you will be at your computer with dictionaries readily available. Take notes and expand your vocabulary. It is humbling to realize how much you do not know and how much you can learn – and there is also tremendous pleasure in it.

In-depth reading. In addition to online reading, focus on reading as much literature in your target language as you can. Also, if your budget allows, subscribe to the print edition of a foreign periodical. It will not only help you keep up with your language, but it will also help you feel more immersed and more connected to the language, which is essential.

Total immersion. Spending some time in a country where your source (or target) language is spoken is ideal. However, this can be cost-prohibitive and might not always be realistic. Try to make it a priority as often as your budget permits.

Language clubs. Spending time with native or near-native speakers of the language you would like to keep active is a good way to keep the momentum going. Find a group of people and get together for your French afternoon chat, German lunch, etc. Occasionally, language learners, mostly beginners, will hear about these groups and think that they are a fantastic way to practice the language and learn grammar. Gently remind them that the group is not meant as a language acquisition program, but as a way for active, fluent speakers to keep their skills current. It is no fun explaining basic grammar to someone when you would rather be discussing foreign affairs.

Add a word a day to your vocabulary in any language. Subscribe to a word of the day newsfeed and actively try to integrate the word into your everyday vocabulary. This will make you a better translator, interpreter, writer, and public speaker.

CHAPTER 9

❧

GIVING BACK

I've learned that you shouldn't go through life with a catcher's mitt on both hands; you need to be able to throw something back.
—Maya Angelou

The American poet and novelist Maya Angelou said it very well, and her message applies to many aspects of professional and personal life. We all want to succeed in our businesses, we want to be recognized for our work, we want to partake in professional development opportunities, and we want to meet and network with our colleagues at conferences and workshops. However, we frequently forget that there are thousands of people working quietly behind the scenes to make these events a reality: colleagues donating their time to professional organizations on the local, regional, national, and international level are the backbone of the professional development side of our business. As opposed to many other professions, where there are for-profit companies that specialize in arranging conferences, usually at exorbitant prices, the translation business is devoid of such organizations. With the exception of small conferences and powwows organized by for-profit sites such as Proz.com (http://www.proz.com/powwows), our industry depends on non-profit organizations for professional development. Do you enjoy belonging to your local chapter? Do you take advantage of workshops and seminars? Are you ready to contribute to making this all happen? If yes, read on. A word of wisdom about time commitment before we get started. None of us really have a lot of time, do we? However, if all of us make even a small time commitment, great things can be accomplished. You do not have to serve on the board of directors of your local organization, but perhaps you can make some phone calls to recruit more members, or maybe you can proofread the organization's newsletter for an hour or two every quarter. There is no magic number, and showing up is a great start. Without you, there would be no chapters nor organizations.

The importance of professional organizations

Imagine, for a moment, if you will, the following scenario: there is no American Translators Association, no UNIVERSITAS Austria Interpreters' and Translators' Association, no Federal Association of Interpreters and Translators in Germany (BDÜ), no Institute of Translation and Interpreting (ITI) in the U.K., nor any of the other valuable associations around the world. What would that mean for the profession? Could you imagine a world without certified translators, court interpretation certifications, and advocacy groups? Every professional group, whether it be lawyers, internet marketers, veterinarians, or actors has a professional association. In our case, all these groups and associations are largely made up by volunteers. While it is convenient to think that there are plenty of others to help our associations by volunteering, it really is not true. Others might think that you should be in charge and you might think that yet another person should be in charge. We should collectively stop trying to hand off responsibility to others and take action ourselves. Most of these organizations are regularly in need of more volunteers and active board members. Think about how much these organizations have done for you in terms of professional development, the professional credibility you gain by listing yourself as a member of the organization, and invaluable networking opportunities with colleagues, potential employers, or new contacts. The networking and business possibilities are very valuable and for us, joining the board of directors of our regional and national organizations, respectively, has not only been a huge commitment but also a challenge, delight, and honor. We truly believe that you should give back to the community at large in some way, whether it is profession-specific or not, and getting involved with your local or regional chapter certainly is a good way to start. There is a reason that the U.S. has a very high percentage of individuals doing volunteer work, higher than anywhere else in the world: Americans believe in giving back. While the pro bono work rates are not as high elsewhere in the world, do not let that stop you. Go ahead and get started!

Finding the right task

Once you have decided that you would like to help your chapter, contact the board of directors of the organization, whose members and e-mail addresses are usually listed on the organization's website. You can be quite certain that the board will be more than happy to hear from you.

There are hundreds of tasks – small and large – that you can take on to help your local, state, or national organization. If you are not sure how you would like to contribute, here are some ideas that should help you get started. Not all organizations might have the need for each of these tasks, so pick a few things that are a good fit for your skills and abilities and then approach the board.

- Serving on the organization's professional development committee.

- Helping organize an annual event, such as a holiday party or an international translation day celebration.

- Finding and/or booking rooms for the organization's events, or just one event, as needed.

- Supplying, storing, and keeping track of required meeting materials, such as banners, paperwork, pens, sign-in sheets, etc.

- Serving as liaison for any out-of-town presenters speakers or guests that the organization has invited.

- Doing fundraising for the organization.

- Serving as the organization's webmaster.

- Maintaining the organization's member database and adding new members as they join the organization.

- Serving as the organization's e-mail communications liaison, sending all communications on behalf of the organization to its members and interested parties.

- Finding and testing new software useful for linguists and telling colleagues about it either via a newsletter, e-mail or online forum.

- Writing articles for the organization's monthly/quarterly newsletter.

- Proofreading the newsletter before it is sent out to all members.

- Contributing ideas for articles to the newsletter.

- Agreeing to be interviewed for a newsletter article.

- Writing press releases for the organization that will be sent out to media and posted on the website.

- Helping compose flyers and handouts announcing meetings, workshops and other events.

- Writing and/or maintaining the organization's blog.

- Creating and printing certificates of attendance for workshop attendees.

- Writing thank-you letters and other official correspondence on behalf of the organization.

- Assisting the treasurer with payment processing and other duties.

- Managing the chapter's online payment processing service, ensuring payments are received and processed properly.

- Filing the organization's taxes.

- Helping brainstorm and/or creating a logo for the organization.

- Designing the layout for the group's website.

- Volunteering as photographer during all or any one of the events so the images can be used in print and online.

- Designing a letterhead template to be used for official communications.

- Boosting membership by making a presentation to a local group of professionals in any industry.

- Approaching fellow professional organizations about working with your chapter to achieve common goals.

- Volunteering your time to other chapters and groups that come to your town to have meetings of events.

- Creating/revising bylaws, code of ethics or other rules of the organization.

Serving on the board of directors

The most significant way that you can contribute to the organization's success is by serving on its board of directors, which is a major commitment in terms of time and effort. Many chapter and groups have specific requirements as to who is elegible to serve on the board. Most chapters and groups have job descriptions, which you can request for your review. This will give you a very precise idea of what is expected of you and you will then be able to determine if you can make the commitment that is required of you. Many organizations hold board member elections once a year, and new members need to formally present their candidacy, run for office, and be elected. In most cases, few people run opposed. Other organizations are more informal and simply appoint board members during board meetings. Be sure to inquire about the process with your local group or chapter.

If you are ready to be on the board of directors, you might serve as:

- President

- Vice-President

- Secretary

- Treasurer

- Membership Director

- PR Director

- Professional Development Director

- Ethics Director

- Newsletter Editor

- Other functions as needed

Many organizations have different directors and co-directors specific to their needs. If you are ready to be on the board of directors but are not quite sure you can handle an entire committee/section by yourself, consider becoming a co-director.

Professional responsibility and time commitment

Even though you will not be paid for the work you do for the organization, you have to consider any job that is assigned to you a professional obligation. This means that when you agree to take on a project, you will be expected, mainly by the board of directors, to do it and to report back. Do not take on projects or responsibilities that you do not think you can handle, as you will be doing the organization a disfavor. You are under no obligation to accept a particular task, but once you do, you will be expected to complete it. Saying no to any job that is not within your abilities or area of expertise or that you simply cannot handle is completely acceptable.

The time commitment will vary greatly, depending on how active the organization is, how long it has existed, the level of organization and many other factors. Traditionally, be prepared to spend more time when the organization is younger and has a lot of foundation-building to do. There is no real number in terms of how many hours you will spend, but many organizations expect their board members to put in 3-5 hours a week. We have been working around 5-10 hours a week for our organizations, and while it is a substantial amount or work, it is also very rewarding. Do not feel guilty if all you can commit to is two hours a month to help organize a get-together: anything that you can do for the organization, preferably on a consistent basis, will be appreciated. Remember that you will not necessarily have to put in work every day, but that during certain times, your entire day might be taken up by association business. Such is the case for us, as we both edit our organizations' newsletters, resulting in a substantial time commitment of several 10-hour days.

If you do accept a position or take on a responsibility that you cannot give the attention and time it deserves, this will affect you professionally. So do yourself a favor and take a hard look at the responsibilities you can assume and those you cannot. No is a powerful word.

How to start your own translation and interpretation organization

This section is based on a lengthy article originally written by Judy and Karen M. Tkaczyk that was published in the American Translators Association's Chronicle magazine in June 2009 under the title "Lessons from Nevada: Establishing a Local Translator/Interpreter Organization." The content is reprinted with the permission of the co-author, Karen M. Tkaczyk, and Jeff Sanfacon, who edits the *Chronicle*.[1] The article chronicles the Nevada Interpreters and Translators As-

---

1   Judy A. Jenner and Karen M. Tkaczyk, "Lessons from Nevada: Establishing a Local Translator/Interpreter Organization," ATA Chronicle (June 2009): 16 – 19. The article has been significantly shortened and adapted to fit the format of this book. Reprinted with permission of the ATA Chronicle and Karen M. Tkaczyk.

sociation's journey from a bold idea to an actual association with bylaws, a board of directors, monthly board meetings, a top-notch website, many professional development opportunities throughout the state, and rapidly growing membership numbers. While most of the following ideas are based on how to start an association in the U.S., many of the lessons, with the exceptions of taxation and other details, can be applied universally.

If you have been disheartened by the lack of a translator and interpreter association in your area, state, or country, now is the time to change it. After you finish this section, you will see that it is very possible to start your own thriving association with just a handful of highly motivated people.

Case study: lessons from Nevada

Establishing a regional translators and interpreters association is not an unmanageable task. With a little organization, several highly committed professionals, and a lot of determination, establishing a local or regional association is a very achievable goal.

The basics

&. **Research.** The first task is to find out if there is already an organization of this type in the state/region. Is there significant interest in this type of group among professionals in the area? Contact national organizations and ask if they have any contacts in your area. What challenges did these organizations face when establishing their groups? Consider both interpreter- and translator-specific organizations, and try to obtain information on whether anyone else has attempted this in your area.

&. **Learn from other organizations:** Nevada is a very large state, and we would eventually like to have active sections in both southern (Las Vegas) and northern (Reno, Carson City) Nevada, and even in the outlying areas at some point. The Carolina Association of Translators and Interpreters (CATI) has been most kind in advising us on how their organization works well over a large region. Other organizations, such as the Northern California Translators Association (NCTA), have also helped out by sharing their experiences and lending advice about how to get started. The main thing is to not be afraid to ask for help. This is a very friendly industry and colleagues are frequently delighted to offer assistance.

&. **Create a good team:** An organization is only going to be as good as its team members. You do not need many: a few very committed people will be enough in the beginning.

Write bylaws: This process can be an intimidating task, particularly if no one on the team has previous experience. Start by reading the bylaws of other associations, which can usually be found on their websites. These can provide you with a basic template for how such documents should be structured. Remember that bylaws are not meant to be set in stone. Therefore, it is important to include a provision in the bylaws allowing for changes to be made as necessary.

State administration: Incorporate in your state. Of course, the process varies, so find out what your state requires and collect the necessary paperwork. We needed items such as bylaws, records of meetings, and copies of our promotional materials. Once we were approved for 501(c)6 status (see next item), we had to follow up with our state department of taxation.

Taxation issues: In the U.S., translation and interpreting professional associations fall into the category of business leagues and are eligible for tax exemption under the 501(c)6 status. Check with your local taxation office if you live in another country. NITA had a growth phase where several founding members were in favor of our association becoming a 501(c)3 association (a charity), but with ATA's advice and after reading of IRS documents on the subject, the board reached a consensus to file for 501(c)6 status. You should note that there is a 15-month period from the date of incorporation during which it is best to file Form 1024. There are possible ways around this for those who are not sure they can file within this period, but that timeline was not too hard for us to meet.

Board Management

Create a board of directors: This is the most crucial element to the organization's success. You should be realistic. Your core people will be doing all the work, at least initially. In the beginning, try to recruit two or three officers. Ideally, you will have a president, vice-president, treasurer, secretary, and perhaps others with specific roles (e.g., professional development, membership, or public relations). NITA started out with just six people. Be sure to invite people to the board who are committed to helping the organization grow, and who are not afraid of rolling up their sleeves.

Establish criteria for board officers: Who would you like to have on the board? Professional translators or interpreters only? Students? Corporations? Decide what works for you. In our case, we have professional translators and interpreters, and one translation student, who have all worked in the profession for several years. We invite prospective board members to send us their résumés and tell us why they would like to join the board and what they could contribute. We have thorough "job descriptions" to help people understand what each role involves, and encourage all members to attend board meetings to see how the association functions.

❧ **Establish ground rules for expectations:** How many hours are you expecting board members to put in? By setting expectations, fellow language professionals will be able to decide if serving on the board or on a committee is something they will be able to fit into their schedules.

Membership

❧ **Determine a membership fee structure.** Will you have student members? Corporate memberships? Discounted memberships? We went with $35 for a basic membership, as we are a very young organization. We also have student and corporate memberships.

❧ **Recruit members.** We looked at ATA's directory listings for Nevada and wrote notes to all the members in our area, encouraging them to join NITA. In addition, we contacted as many other translator/interpreter organizations as we could.

Building the foundation

❧ **Open a bank account.** The treasurer is the one who should handle the finances and have authorization to sign checks on behalf of the organization. Be sure to keep all organization finances separate from any personal finances.

❧ **Board meetings.** In the bylaws, you will have decided the minimum number of board meetings to hold each year and minimum attendance requirements for board members.

❧ **Read *Robert's Rules of Order.*** This is another of the "do not reinvent the wheel" concepts. Robert's Rules (www.robertsrules.org) are the standard for how to run board meetings, hold votes, make motions, etc. Understanding them is a great way to hold efficient and productive meetings.

❧ **Decide how you will communicate.** This was somewhat of a challenge for us. We needed to decide which e-mail addresses to use, and whether webmail or direct configuration was most effective and secure. Thanks to our information technology guru, we all have @nitaonline.org addresses as well as our other business e-mails we use. We also have a great online forum called The Cantina, where board members can exchange ideas. It is separate from e-mail, and we all have to remember to go there several times a week, since our organization moves pretty fast. Once we figured out the best way to handle e-mail communications -- who should receive which e-mails, who does not need to be copied -- we were able to control the sometimes overwhelming flow of e-mails and replies and streamline the process.

Create a good website/find an information technology guru. The website does not have to be fancy, and can contain just the basics (About/ Contact Us/Board/Events). A basic site can be set up with Google Sites (which can also host the domain for roughly $10/year). Ideally, you should have associated e-mail addresses for each member. If your budget permits, hiring an information technology person to help you with the site is ideal. If not, try to find a board member with these skills.

Added Value

Design a logo. We chose a simple design with our state's outline and our organization's name inside of it. We were able to use our personal networks to receive several free concept submissions from people with graphic design skills, and offered a free membership to anyone whose design was chosen.

ATA affiliation: Most new organizations cannot meet the requirements for becoming an ATA chapter, but becoming an ATA affiliate group has less taxing requirements. NITA quickly achieved affiliate status (please visit the American Translators Association Chapters and Groups Information at www.atanet.org/chaptersandgroups/index.php).

Raise money: Membership dues will most likely not be enough to keep your organization afloat in the beginning. Raise money by offering workshops and, if possible, have the speaker donate his or her time. Tracy Young, NITA's founder and immediate past president, donated 40 hours of her time to do a very popular health care interpreting training class, which we offered at a very affordable rate.

Publish a newsletter: We simply created our newsletter in Microsoft Publisher, which comes with the regular suite of Microsoft Office products, and sent it out as a PDF. The newsletter is not fancy, but it is a great way to communicate with members. Some of us also regularly contribute to other association publications, and ask to reprint some of their articles so that the newsletter can have a wide range of contributions.

Offer professional development: This is one of the most important functions of a professional association. In our first year, NITA offered two types of interpreting training, and the board has some form of continuing planned or ongoing education planned at least every quarter in 2009. Of course, we are always looking for excellent and affordable speakers who do not break our piggy bank. While we do not like to do it, sometimes we have to ask folks to donate their time, which many gladly do.

Create brochures/marketing material: While this can really cut into your budget, you can at least make simple tri-fold pamphlets that can be printed at the local office supply store, preferably in color. We have a large banner with the organization's name on it, and we hang it on the wall wherever meetings or events are held.

Public relations: Ideally, you will be pitching to local and regional newspapers, television and radio stations, and other media outlets and asking them to profile the organization. Alternatively, you can send out free press releases about your organization online and write about it as much as you can -- on translation blogs, Twitter, Facebook, etc. Use social media to get the word out about your organization. Add it to your LinkedIn profile. You can also start a LinkedIn group and post on the discussion boards.

It just takes work

Establishing a regional translators and interpreters association is not an unmanageable task. Once the work is split between several people whose skills complement each other, the core group can achieve a great deal. Of course, for a thriving organization, a broader membership is needed. NITA had nearly 40 members at the end of our first year, largely in northern Nevada. Our big task for 2009 was growing the organization in the Las Vegas area and beginning to hold events there, which we have already achieved.Karen is NITA president for 2009-2011, and Judy is NITA's vice-president for 2009-2011. We have no doubt that the hard work of all the association's volunteers will continue to pay off, and that as a group we will meet our goals of elevating the profession in our state.

CHAPTER 10

§≥

WORK/LIFE BALANCE

As self-employed entrepreneurs, we benefit from all the fantastic advantages of being our own boss. For those of us who have worked in the corporate world, either as linguists or in another position, shifting to being self-employed is a major change, and usually a great one. The U.S. economy is driven, in large part, by hundreds of thousands of small businesses and self-employed professionals, and being one of them is very powerful. According to the U.S. Census Bureau's 2002 survey of small-business owners, approximately half of all U.S. businesses are home-based, no-employee businesses. However, being self-employed comes with the enormous responsibility of having to carry all the burden of every aspect of a business, many of which are assumed by employers in a traditional work relationship, including accounting, payroll, marketing, promotions, business development, and IT. There is a long list of pros and cons to running your own business. It is not for everyone, and a large majority of small businesses fail in the first few years for a variety of reasons.

Pros of being an entrepreneur

When looking at our own professional lives, it is quite easy to come up with many aspects that we love about it. We will discuss the pros before we look at the downsides of being your own boss. This list is intended to give you a good overview of both sides of the equation if you are still trying to decide whether to go out on your own.

If you have decided to be your own boss and to run your freelance translation or interpretation business full-time or part-time: congratulations! Give yourself a well-deserved pat on the back. Most employees dream of running their own businesses, but relatively few ever have the courage, the skills, and the drive to do so. This is a fantastic opportunity, but also a big challenge: no risk, no reward.

Making your own schedule

When informally surveying our friends and colleagues, making their own schedule tops the list of what linguists like best about being self-employed. That is not surprising, since the ability to control one's own time truly is a fantastic perk. Those of us who have left highly structured work environments – and by that we mean strict hierarchies, long (but not always efficient) meetings, needless power struggles over projects, etc. – appreciate the flexibility of working for ourselves. Now there is no need to start the work day at 8 a.m. if you are not a morning person and prefer to work until 2 a.m. You do not have to sit in front of your computer, merely being physically present at work when there is not much to do. There is no need to limit your personal e-mailing time to after-work hours. You do not need to hurry back from your lunch break so your boss can see you in your office: welcome to entrepreneurship! You are your own boss, and you are responsible exclusively to yourself and to your clients.

In terms of scheduling work hours, there are many different philosophies. Some linguists like keeping regular office hours in their time zone, while others suggest holding office hours in the time zone of their main clients, which is especially relevant if most of your clients work overseas. We are strong believers that there is no specific schedule that will work for everyone. You are self-employed for a reason, so you get to choose your schedule. You do not have to force yourself into a schedule that works for others but might not be ideal for you. Take a look at your habits and your preferences, and design your schedule in such a way that you maximize your productivity, which will be different for everyone. For instance, Judy is not much of a morning person, and having to be at work at 8:30 a.m. on the other side of town was always a challenge for her. It took her a while to realize that now she really is in control of her time and her schedule, and that there is no reason to feel bad if she is not in front of her computer at 8:30 a.m. After all, she does work every morning until 2 a.m. or so, because that is her most productive time. Some people take a tremendous amount of comfort in having a set schedule, but we like to be flexible with ours. If someone invites us to lunch, we go. If we feel like taking a kickboxing class at 3 p.m., we do. A nap at 11 a.m.? Why not? Remember that you now have 24 hours to accomplish what you traditionally had to accomplish in eight hours. You can split up that time any way you like, while working around your clients' schedules and their wishes. However, if a client wants to be able to reach you during regular business hours while working on a particular project for him or her, you should go to great lengths to accommodate them. Always answer your cell phone when you are away from the office, and return all missed call as promptly as you can. Freelancing is also an ideal way to combine a profession with children because of linguists' ability to have a flexible schedule.

Your own dress code

Most freelancers really enjoy the ability to work in whatever clothes they like and not having to adhere to a corporate dress code. After managing the Spanish-language translation team for an e-commerce company for many years, Judy now understands why it was so difficult to recruit full-time translators: it was a hard sell to get linguists out of their comfortable clothes and their home offices. The beauty of the online work world is that you can constantly communicate with clients and colleagues, but unless you want them to, they will not be able to see you, hence enabling you to work in whatever clothes you want. This will also save you money, and depending on the dress code your previous employer had, that amount can be quite significant. It is time to dismiss the traditional notion of professional dress. This is a challenge for many of us who have worked in corporate environments, which traditionally have been relatively rigid. Throughout the years, it also has conditioned professionals like us to equate professional dress with professional work, which is not necessarily true anymore. While some linguists feel more in work mode when they are dressed professionally, for others this is not important. Personally, we like getting dressed first thing after we get up, hence signaling to ourselves that the work day has begun (at whatever time that is). Do not let anyone tell you that you should do this one way or another: there is no right or wrong, and not an approach that fits everyone. It is time to rethink the traditional work model in many, many ways.

No wasted time in meetings

This will sound familiar to anyone who has worked in a formal corporate environment: long meetings, during which you try to reach consensus among a group of people, many times on issues of no consequence. Many people would not even pay attention during meetings, because they would busy themselves with their handheld devices, thus making the meeting even more challenging for all parties. At some point, this led a project manager at one of Judy's previous companies to collect all devices in a basket prior to the meeting. It is sad that it had to come to that point, but it worked. If you are like us, you might prefer doing actual work to sitting around talking about it (and possibly playing with your handheld device). Some meetings are very important and necessary – but we will go out on a limb to say that is the minority of meetings. We do not have any of these interruptions in the forms of meetings, and we are more efficient because of that. However, if we do have meetings with clients, which are an important part of the service we provide, we can take all the time required, even if it takes all day. When it comes to making internal company decisions, we make them quickly and efficiently. Since it is only the two of us, we do not have to do any of the things we had grown accustomed to in large companies: making sure no one's foot gets stepped on, respecting political boundaries, standing up for your department, etc. All these things have little to do with the work that needs to be accomplished, and when they are stripped away, a small organization is much more nimble and effective.

No more cubicles

While having an office full of cubicles is the most efficient way to use office space in large buildings, they also tend to be detrimental to morale. It goes without saying that not everyone can have an office, but cubicles are quite restrictive. They make you feel as if you entire life has been reduced to this small space with a chair, a computer, a shelf, perhaps a few potted plants, some framed pictures, and no privacy. In the beginning, you think you will never get used to working in a cubicle, especially if you had an office in a previous position, but the human body and mind are incredibly adaptable. Still, a cubicle is quite confining and is typically not a place suited to creative work. After working in the corporate world, rethinking the office space can be challenging, but break free of the preconceived notions that you have to work in a specific, limited space, and find a spot that works for you, whether that is on your bedroom floor, in your sunroom, on your porch, or at your kitchen table. You do not have to sit at a table with a straight-backed office chair. Look at it as the office life of the new millennium: you get to make the rules.

No more co-workers

While we have made lifelong friendships in corporate environments, negotiating the intricate and delicate web of social codes and possible hidden agendas can be tricky. Our co-workers have traditionally been wonderful people who strive to achieve a common goal. Most offices that have very little conflict, but as a general rule, the more people you get together in a corporate environment, the more room there is for error and interpersonal conflict. If your co-workers were not your favorite part of your previous jobs: congratulations! Now you have none, unless you really want to, and you get to choose them. If you miss them, you know where to find them and can always meet them for lunch.

Your very own democracy

When we were still employees working for companies owned and managed by someone else, sometimes supervisors would come to us with odd ideas that they wanted us to help implement. When asked, we would politely give our opinion on these projects. Most of the time, it was to no avail, as our opinion was not relevant and we were simply expected to help implement the project. This is typical of a traditional employee-employer relationship: you will have to work on certain things that do not fall into your area of expertise, that do not make any sense, or that just seem like a waste of time and resources. As an entrepreneur, you get to decide which projects to work on. That being said, if one of your trusted repeat customers asks you to implement a project you do not think is in the client's best interest, you should, as a professional vendor, point that out to the client. If they decide to proceed with the project in spite of your professional advice, you still have the option of declining the project, which you certainly do not have as an employee. However, strike a balance between being a trustworthy and reliable vendor and an outside assessor who chimes in with too much unsolicited advice.

Choosing your clients

In addition to being able to choose your projects, you also get to choose your clients. You are under no professional obligation to accept a project from a customer who approaches you for a quote. However, once you give the client a formal quote and he/she accepts it, then you must comply with the terms of the quote. If the customer does not accept the quote and proposes amendments (on price, delivery, payment terms, etc.), then the original quote is no longer valid and you do not have to accept the new terms or the job. Freelance linguists often feel they have to accept every project, but we do not. If a project sounds too good to be true, it probably is. One of your main objectives is to protect your business, to limit your liabilities and to prevent uncollectable invoices. Hence, if a potential customer raises red flags for you, listen to your inner voice. There are a wide variety of excellent tools to use in order to research the payment record of translation agencies, such as Payment Practices (www.paymentpractices.net), which is expertly run by our colleague Ted Wozniak. However, these fantastic databases contain no information on direct clients. If you cannot find any solid information on the company, that is a bad sign. If companies are e-mailing you from free e-mail accounts (such as Yahoo or Gmail), that should raise a flag for you. When dealing with individuals who want to get documents translated, it is an entirely different story: many individuals do not have a substantial online footprint, nor are they very tech-savvy, which does not mean that they are unreliable in terms of payment, but you have no way of knowing. When in doubt, ask for full payment or a partial deposit up front.

Choosing how much to work

How much you work, and consequently, how much you earn, is completely up to you. If you want to work only part-time while taking care of your children, you certainly can. If you want to accept as many projects as you can during a given month to save money for a vacation, do it. Speaking of vacation: go whenever you would like, but be mindful of informing your clients and colleagues ahead of time so they know your schedule and can plan accordingly. A good idea is to send out a message to your contacts (blind-copying everyone) to inform them of your upcoming vacation. If you get up on a Monday and do not feel like working at all, program an out-of-office message and take the day off. You do not have to ask anyone for permission, fill out a permission slip, nor do you have to feel guilty: it is your own business, so enjoy it. However, your clients should always be first, so take care of any pending projects before you take time off. Communication with your customers is key, so keep them informed of your timelines. And stop feeling guilty about taking time off: you are the boss!

Cons of being an entrepreneur

Now that we have looked at some of the positives of being a small-business owner, we must look at the other side of the coin. There also is a long list of cons to entrepreneurship to keep in mind.

Becoming a workaholic

Being able to set your own schedule is both a blessing and a curse. Most linguists inherently know that they have to strike a good work-life balance, but sometimes we get very excited about the money we can make by packing our schedules as tightly as possible. That is not always a good idea, especially in the long run. We know of several linguists who work so much that they barely leave the house and have very little social interaction. You can read more about that topic in the social isolation section of this chapter. Just because you can work around the clock does not mean that you should. Be kind to yourself and schedule some time off whenever it is convenient for you. Some linguists like to go into workaholic-mode for several months in order to take a few months off afterward. Whatever you do, make some time for leisure activities and for regrouping. Try simply turning off the computer, which is easier said than done. As home-based entrepreneurs, we are never really off duty, but turning off the computer is a good way to signal to yourself and other people that you are officially not working. Having the computer turned off will not only ensure that you get out into the real world or at least into your backyard, but it will also help you save the planet and your wallet by lowering the power bill. Plus, that poor machine works very hard and deserves an occasional break.

Irregular income

The lack of regular income is one of the greatest deterrents for would-be entrepreneurs, not only in our profession. The inability to predict future earnings can be very frightening, and it puts a lot of stress on entrepreneurs. Business is often cyclical, and no matter how much you try to plan, you will not be able to predict how much you will be making in any given month. Hence, you should have at least a little bit of a financial cushion before you go out on your own. Put away money in savings if you have extra earnings in any particular month. When business is booming, pretend that you will not have any income the following month (which might or might not happen) and plan accordingly. Be conservative. Even when you have repeat customers, you never know if they will be around the next month. Before you go out on your own, you need to confront the financial reality of having irregular income. If you get nervous just reading about this, you are better off having a solid financial cushion of at least six months' income saved up before you start your own business. There is no need to add to the anxiety that already comes with venturing into unknown territory.

Also, consider that you will only get paid for the time that you actually spend working on customers' projects. No one will pay you for the time you spend marketing, doing your accounting, meeting with potential customers, etc. If you do not think you can handle the pressure of not having regular, predictable income, then running your own business might not be the best choice for you.

The constant client acquisition process

Finding new business is one of the great challenges of any entrepreneur, regardless of the profession or industry. While having a solid list of existing clients is fantastic and very important, you have no way of controlling or predicting whether they will still be your customers next month. Companies fold, get sold, your contact person might leave the company or retire, and new vendors might be hired, so do not rely on your current customers to be your permanent customer base. Ideally, they would be, but just like you, they have no contractual commitment to use your services for every project, unless you have signed a long-term collaboration agreement. Hence, you need to continuously find more work to ensure future earnings. This is quite a time-consuming undertaking, and it will never end – as long as you have your business, you must work on acquiring new clients. If you do not think this is for you, rethink your strategy and perhaps partner with a colleague who is more interested in business development than you are and is willing to do the majority of the work in that area.

Lack of health insurance and other benefits

This is a big downside to being an entrepreneur, mainly in the U.S. While not all employers offer health insurance benefits to their full-time employees, many of them do, which is a significant part of the reason people strive for full-time employment even though they would prefer to be self-employed. It is an unfortunate reality of the American marketplace that many would-be entrepreneurs are discouraged from going out on their own because they would not be able to get health care benefits for themselves and/or their families. While it is possible to buy your own policy from a leading provider or to join an organization such as a chamber of commerce to qualify for a group rate, these insurance plans are typically much more expensive than the policies you can obtain through an employer. When calculating the cost, risk, and benefits of going into business for yourself, you must take the cost of health care into account. In addition, you will have no paid sick leave, paid holidays or any other paid time off. Many other countries, especially European nations, have government-run health plans for the self-employed, which entrepreneurs pay into. These plans get more expensive as one earns more, but they ensure that all entrepreneurs can get coverage.

Computer-induced maladies

While computers are a blessing for our profession – could you imagine typing your translations on a typewriter with no electronic resources? – they are also the cause of many physical ailments, including carpal tunnel and eye problems. You might have these problems whether you are an entrepreneur or not, as most professionals spend the vast majority of their days in front of the computer. But if you are working for yourself, you might be even more prone to spending time in front of the computer in an effort to run a profitable business. While this is certainly commendable, listen to what the experts have to say and take regular breaks away from your computer, get some exercise, let your eyes wander into the distance, and do some wrist stretches. If you type slowly, have a significant amount of typing to, or want to save your wrists from excessive typing, try speech recognition software such as Dragon Naturally Speaking (http://www.nuance.com/naturallyspeaking/). The international version of the software works with many languages, and you will have to train it to recognize your voice and speech patterns. It is not a perfect tool (yet), but it can greatly increase your efficiency and reduce stress on your wrists by eliminating a significant amount of typing.

Too many e-mails

This problem is not unique to entrepreneurs, but if you are self-employed, you will not respond to all e-mails yourself (unless you have staff). You have to deal with every message at some point, preferably no later than one day after receiving it. You might receive hundreds of e-mails each day, which can become quite overwhelming. Try to establish a sensible order of importance, which will help you determine which e-mails need to be answered immediately and which can wait. One approach is to answer current customers' messages first, followed by potential customers' and then colleagues' messages. If you feel that you have so many e-mail messages that it is impossible to catch up with all of them, take 15 to 30 minutes every day to empty your inbox. Create inbox folders for the e-mails you want to keep.

Too many customer requests

If you are already self-employed, this scenario will be familiar to you: some days, nothing happens and you wonder if the phone will ever ring again or if you will ever get another e-mail from a potential customer. The very next day, you find yourself working on a large rush project and you are inundated with potential customers requesting quotes for projects. Sometimes it will feel like there is not enough time in your day to take care of all these things, and that is normal. Business has a tendency to happen all at the same time, and when things are slow, they are really slow. Use the slow time to relax and prepare yourself for the times when you will be working 14 hours a day. You can choose to turn down business whenever you want, but try to accept as many projects as are feasible in the time frame that you have available. But be sure not to overpromise; overdeliver instead.

Lack of motivation

Since you are reading this book, you are either self-employed or are very seriously thinking about becoming self-employed. Usually, the folks who take this step are highly motivated and do not need a boss to tell them to get to work. However, there will be times when it might be difficult to get motivated, especially when business is slow. No one will force you to get out of bed on a day when you do not have much business, so you need to have enough self-discipline to give yourself the proverbial kick in the behind to get up and tackle your day. If you cannot come up with the motivation you need to run your business, no one will.

No accountability to anyone other than yourself

The only person inside your company you are accountable to is yourself or yourself and your business partner if you have one. You also need to be accountable to your clients, but ultimately, you are the one who is calling the shots and running the business. While it is wonderful to be able to control all aspects of your business, it can also quickly lead to poor business decisions, as you have all the discretion in the world. Entrepreneurship is best suited for those with a high sense of responsibility, self-motivation, and drive to succeed.

Social isolation

Social isolation, often brought on by spending too much time at home by yourself, can be a significant problem for many home-based freelancers. Often, as freelance linguists we get so comfortable in our online world and our familiar surroundings that it almost feels as if there is no need to leave the house and interact with people in person. However, having real social contacts is essential to our wellbeing, and also to keep us grounded and focused on something other than work. Many linguists make the switch from full-time in-house translator or interpreter to full-time entrepreneur. Oftentimes, it is very refreshing to have peace and quiet and to not have any co-workers around. One is in her own space, with her own rules, her own music on the radio, with no one looking over her shoulder. However, this can also be a significant downside and can contribute to translators being considered, unfairly, as eccentric and anti-social. With no co-workers around, for better or for worse, taking your focus off our work and making small talk, you will quickly realize that you might spend your entire day without speaking to anyone. While some of the social interactions in traditional work environments can be irritating, they do provide nice breaks and balance to our lives. If you are living with a spouse, significant other or have a family, social isolation will not be much of an issue for you. However, many young professionals are single when they start their careers and need to be sure to integrate some social activities into their lives. While virtual contact is fantastic, and many of us have built up substantial support networks online, there simply is no substitute for real human contact where you can read your friend's facial expression and share a cup of coffee or a glass of wine at happy hour.

Fighting social isolation

Here are some suggestions for what you can do to avoid becoming too much of a homebody.

> **Keep weekly appointments.** Perhaps you used to get together with a friend for lunch or a movie every week before you made the switch to your entrepreneurial life? If you have always been an entrepreneur, keeping weekly appointments with friends (or clients, or clients-to-be) will give your schedule some structure and get you out of the house. Having weekly get-togethers with friends and former co-workers is a good way to get away from the computer and get some one-on-one time with real people. If you

do not have the time or do not want to spend time and money on a proper meal, grab a quick cup of coffee with a friend at your favorite local coffee shop. Many cafés offer free wireless internet, so you could also do some work before or after meeting your friend.

Find a workout buddy. Commit to doing something for your physical health on a regular basis. Having this kind of appointment not only gets you out of the house, but it also allows you to spend some time with a friend while doing something healthy and not straining your budget. There is no need to belong to a fancy gym: you can simply go for a walk in the park, play tennis at a public park, go for a short hike, or meet at the local swimming pool. For more information, please see the fitness section of this chapter.

Walk your dog. If you have a dog bigger than a Chihuahua, then you should be walking it on a daily basis. Perhaps you have a neighbor who wants to go with you? Then you could combine walking your dogs with exercise and catching up. Dog parks are also a great place for a mid-afternoon break with your four-legged friend. And you never know whom you could meet. Business sometimes originates in unexpected places, and stranger things have happened than meeting a future client at the dog park.

Go out for lunch. One of the benefits of being an entrepreneur is that you can eat lunch at home rather than in the lunchroom or at an overpriced restaurant, which is both healthier and more affordable. However, when you do not see people all day, it can get quite lonely, so set up lunch dates with a friend once or twice a week. Some people might think that being entrepreneurs means that we have unlimited time and can easily drive to the other side of town for a quick lunch. We usually explain to friends and former co-workers that we do not have the benefit of a paid lunch hour, and that this time is all opportunity cost for us. This usually makes sense to them and we settle for somewhere in the middle. Your time is the only resource you have, so be sure to use it wisely.

Take your laptop out of the house. If you have a laptop, you are in luck: you do not have to physically sit at your desk when working. You are your own boss, so you can work anywhere you want. Ideally, your destination would have wireless internet, but depending on the project you are working on (say, you are in the proofing stages of a translation), you will not even need that. You could sit in a park, your backyard, a café, the library, or any place you like. Sometimes it is nice to leave the house with work in tow, because now you can enjoy some social contact while working. And it is pretty amazing to sit in a café in the middle of the afternoon, dressed casually, working away on your laptop, while all the non-entrepreneurs are slaving away in an office, dressed in formal business attire and going to pointless meetings. If you take your laptop out of your office a lot, consider integrating a simple marketing strategy: buy a laptop skin, which you can customize with your logo. Get started at http://schtickers.com. You might be surprised how many people will come up to you to ask you about your business. The cost for these laptops skins is quite reasonable.

🐾 **Do volunteer work.** Surely you have enough people in your life with whom you want to spend time. However, as a freelancer, you will quickly realize that other people's schedules are not nearly as flexible as yours. You could use some of those flexible hours to do volunteer work when most working-age volunteers are not typically available. Ideally, this would be in a field/area from which you could potentially derive some business. For instance, if you do a lot of work in the social services area, it might be a good idea to do some volunteering for a social service agency. Do not use this solely as a sales opportunity, but when people ask you what you do for a living, and you can certainly tell them that you are a Spanish translator. Your main goal should be to get out of the house, be social, and help the community while you are at it. For more information on pro bono work, please read the giving back chapter.

🐾 **Be accountable to yourself.** So you have not left the house in two days? And you have not changed out of your favorite Snoopy pajamas? While that is very comfortable and your home is probably your castle, you should get out of the house, especially if you are stressed or feeling lonely. When you are on the computer all day without any social interaction, you might tend to overanalyze and overreact to things online (on listservs, translation boards, or terminology discussions). Solely depending on your interactions in cyberspace is not a good way to live. In the long run, being social (on your terms and whenever you want to) is important for your overall health. It also refreshing to get together with people who do not want to talk, in great detail, about the origins of a Greek word and whether it can be used correctly in the final phase of metallurgy production. Sometimes you just have to realize that the world does not revolve ours – or anyone's – profession. Spending time with monolingual friends tends to put things in perspective.

🐾 **Meet your online contacts in person.** While online contacts with colleagues are invaluable, there is no substitute for meeting them in real life. This might be, at times, difficult, depending on where most of your listmates live, but try to meet up during conferences and workshops. Many of these people may have known each other before they started corresponding online, while others might meet in person after a long time of online contact. We try to arrange face-to-face get-togethers with those colleagues with whom we have only interacted in cyberspace. Sometimes it is also worth sending a quick message to the people on the listserv to see who would like to organize a get-together. We have done that quite frequently, and the personal contact has always been fantastic.

Finding a balance

Most of your friends probably work in traditional employee-employer relation-ships and do not take work home with them very frequently. When the clock strikes 5:30 p.m., they might rush out of the office, excited to have the evening to themselves. We remember those times well: after leaving the office, we would have little to worry about until the next day. Now that you have your own busi-ness, things are different. This does not mean that you will have to work through the night and evening every day, but you might need to be available to your cus-tomers at potentially inconvenient times. Your availability for social outings may be a bit unpredictable, which is something that your friends and acquaintances might not always understand. Cancelling a long-planned outing because an im-portant urgent project came up is not ideal, but your business should come first. Hence, saying a polite, but firm "no" to things you cannot commit to is an impor-tant skill. Be sure to explain to your friends and acquaintances the cyclical nature of our work, and that you will have to take projects when they are available to you. You might occasionally miss out on social gatherings, but you will continue building your business. There will be many times when you are not as busy as you would like, and those are great opportunities to catch up with friends and acquaintances that you have not had the chance to see in a while. Just because you are running your own business and have a flexible schedule does not mean you are always available to your friends, and that includes afternoon babysitting for the neighbors and midnight rides to the airport.

The squirrel principle

If you see that a day is shaping up to be quiet after a busy time, during which you hardly left the house, this is the time to powder your nose and meet up with friends. Rather than lamenting the fact that you do not have a project lined up, use the time to catch up on your social activities using the "squirrel" principle – getting your fill of social interaction while you can, so you have some nice memories when you are stuck in front of the computer for 12 hours a day. It would be nice if you could commit to a regular Wednesday night happy hour, but that might not be realistic. Find friends to spend time with you who are also available on short notice. It is quite possible that many of them will be fellow entrepreneurs.

The importance of being fit

Obesity is a significant problem in the industrialized world, no doubt brought on by our sedentary lifestyles and lack of exercise. Translators are no more overweight than other desk-bound professionals, but lack of exercise can be a serious challenge. Since we spend so much time in front of our computers, sometimes getting into a regular exercise routine is not easy. How often have you said to yourself "I do not have time to go for a run/walk/swim/gym?" or "I just need to finish one more page and then I will walk the dog"? It is no secret that lack of exercise will have a negative effect on your health in the long run. You are in the lucky position of having the ability and the opportunity to allocate your time as you see fit. As your own boss, you should strive to be fit and healthy, which will decrease you health care costs and will maximize your productivity. If you have not done any kind of significant physical activity in a while, you need to see your doctor before starting any workout routine. Here are a few tips and pointers on staying fit:

&. **Make an appointment with yourself.** This has been recommended by many fitness gurus, and it usually works. The idea is to treat your workout just like any other appointment that you have scheduled on your calendar, such as client meetings, and sticking to it. If you have to reschedule for any pressing work-related reason, such as a last-minute project, make sure you reschedule this appointment with yourself – just like you would any other appointment. If you are somewhat lax about appointments with yourself, get a personal trainer or simply book a few personal training sessions to get you started. Pretend that not going to the scheduled workout will cut into your bottom line. After all, your health is your business, too!

&. **Find a workout buddy.** For those who find it difficult to be accountable to themselves, finding a workout buddy is the way to go. It could be a fellow entrepreneur or a friend who is on a lunch break from a regular office environment. Whatever the set-up might be, we tend to be less likely to cancel, postpone or feel too lazy to go if there is someone waiting for us to show up. Make it a regular weekly appointment if you can.

&. **Keeping costs low.** As a small-business owner, taking care of your health is certainly important. However, you do not want to invest a lot of money or other valuable resources into getting fit. Contrary to what they tell you on late-night television, you do not have to spend a fortune on DVDs, workout equipment, or join a high-priced gym to do something for your health. For the sake of your wallet, you can keep it simple and inexpensive. Invest in a good pair of shoes and start walking. For a great deal, head to a discount sporting goods store. You can purchase a jump rope for when you do not have time to get out of the house and a few dumbbells to do quick exercises during the day. Many gyms offer low-cost sign-up and monthly fees, especially for women. Since your schedule is flexible, you could pick a plan that allows you to go during non-peak hours, which might be less expensive. Alternatively, consider the local government-supported or non-profit community center, which usually offers classes and gym memberships at significant discounts compared to private gyms. Find an activity or a sport that you really like before investing too much into equipment. The idea is to stay fit while keeping costs low.

Get a dog. It is an old trick you can teach yourself: get a dog, preferably one larger than a Yorkie, one that needs to work off energy and get regular exercise. When Fido comes to try to get you away from your computer, leash in mouth, tail wagging, you will probably head outside with the excited pup. This is good for both you and the your best friend, and having the anxious-looking dog sitting next to your desk will hopefully be enough to motivate you to go outside periodically, even if it is just for a short walk. Your body and your dog will thank you for the regular workout.

Be flexible. Having a set schedule of what you want to do and accomplish is fantastic, but sometimes life intervenes: you get sick, you get the huge project you have been waiting for, you go on vacation, your washer breaks down and you have to wait for the technician – it happens. While you need to be accountable, you should also be flexible. Your plan cannot play out perfectly every week, and rather than stressing about something you cannot plan or could not foresee, simply file it away, and go on with your day. You can go back to working out the next time. A caveat: flexibility should be the exception, not the rule. However, many folks are too ambitious with workouts and have unrealistic schedules (say, six times a week). This tends to have the unfortunate consequence that when life intervenes and messes with the six-times-a-week schedule, people get frustrated and walk away from the exercise plan.

Think long term. Unfortunately, there is no such thing as instant gratification for working out – it is all about the long term. It can be frustrating not to see immediate results, but focus on using the workout as a way to be healthy and happy, not as a way to lose weight or to try to look like Arnold Schwarzenegger. Your physical health will not improve immediately, but this is something you should be doing for life, so find a way to integrate exercise into your life.

🏃 **If you have 5- 15 minutes...** We all know the scenario: we are too busy, the e-mails are piling up, deadlines are coming dangerously closer, and the phone is ringing off the hook. What is the first thing you cancel? Probably your workout. It makes a lot of financial and business sense that your actual work should come first. However, just because you do not have time for a longer workout does not mean you should write the day off in terms of exercise. You could take a quick break from the computer and do 50 jumping jacks. Or do a few push-ups, some sit-ups on an inflatable ball, or a few leg lifts. Run up and down the stairs a few times. Do some stretches while taking a break. Get small dumbbells and do 15 repetitions of a biceps exercise. Do 15 lunges on each leg. There are many easy and effective exercises that you can do in 5-15 minutes without the need for any special equipment. For most of these quick exercises, you do not even have to change into workout clothes. It is a good idea to build breaks into your day and to use the time for some sit-ups or some other quick way of stimulating your muscles. They will thank you once you sit down at the computer for another marathon session. Your body is your temple and your moneymaker, so treat it well.

http://mox.ingenierotraductor.com

© 2010 AMR - Based on a idea by P. Sandford

CHAPTER 11

§⚭

ENTREPRENEURSHIP RECAP

The title of this book has the word "entrepreneurial" in it, and the entire book revolves around the theme of entrepreneurship. This chapter will summarize some of the most important points, introduce some new ideas, and provide a wrap-up. In accordance with what we have discussed throughout the book, you need to get away from thinking like an employee and start thinking like an entrepreneur.

As entrepreneurial linguists, we have to be both entrepreneur and linguist. That does not include having to learn every business strategy overnight – and trust us, you will not – but it simply means that you need to learn and apply several important business lessons. We have outlined some of these lessons, organized by topic, in this book.

Everything we have discussed revolves around entrepreneurship and about how to run your freelance translation (or interpretation) business in such a way that allows you to maximize revenue, quality of life, and hopefully your level of satisfaction with your chosen profession. This all takes time and there is no magic pill that will take you from where you are to the place where you would like to be quickly and effortlessly. The vast majority of successful people have worked very hard to get to where they are, and linguists are no exception. So, if you expect to reach your goals within a few months, you are setting yourself up for disappointment. While it is possible to be successful more quickly than you imagined, that is the exception and not the norm. Some of our colleagues in highly specialized fields with unique marketing plans have found success within a few months, but that is quite unusual.

Let us review the top 20 lessons of this book. Most of them have been covered in-depth in previous chapters, and some are new to provide additional food for thought.

1. Run your business like a business

You are running a legitimate business. Now, start behaving like one. In order to have a successful translation and/or interpretation business, you really should run it full-time. It is difficult, yet not impossible, to run a business like this on the side. We get this question quite frequently from people who want to start out in the business: can I do this on the side? Can I just "pick up a few translation or interpretation projects"? The answer is: you could try it, but it might or might not be feasible. Customers, whether they are direct customers or translation agencies, want to work with vendors who are available and whom they can reach easily. If you are still working full-time at another job, this might be a handicap that you will find challenging to overcome. Would you want to try to do business with someone who is only available after hours? If you are just starting out, perhaps your best bet for moving into the full-time freelance life is joining forces with a more established colleague who would be willing to outsource a few projects to you. If you want to run your own successful business, you should give it all the attention it deserves so it can flourish. We believe it is quite unrealistic to run a thriving business on the side, although there are always exceptions.

2. Welcome to entrepreneurship

It is time to give yourself a well-deserved pat on the back: welcome to entrepreneurship. You are now an entrepreneur. Start defining yourself through that word, and translate it into your language(s). Perhaps you need a sign on your desk reminding you of your entrepreneurial adventure? While you are still a linguist, you are much more than that: you are an entrepreneur and an entrepreneurial linguist. Unfortunately, even if you are a great linguist, if you do not act like an entrepreneur, you might not achieve the monetary success and quality of life you would like. It would be nice if just being a top-notch linguist would ensure an endless supply of business every week for the rest of your working life. But that is not the way the economy works, so you will have to be an entrepreneur first and a linguist second. Find the business, and then put your top-notch language skills to work.

3. A small business is just as legitimate as a big business

We hear that a lot: "I am just a one-person business and I am intimidated by negotiating with a Fortune 500 company!" We understand that it is intimidating, but you need to move away from thinking in those terms. The professionalism and integrity of your business is completely independent of its size. As we have seen in the last few years, just because companies are large certainly does not mean that they are more credible, professional, or ethical. Start developing some pride in your small business status. You might be surprised how refreshing large companies find it to work with smaller enterprises. Judy used to work with leading technology companies when she worked as an in-house translation department manager. She quickly realized that completing projects with these large corporations is really difficult because of their multi-layered hierarchy and the many rounds of approvals and sign-offs. Consider running a small business a competitive advantage and market yourself that way. Think about what bigger businesses (most likely, your customers) like about smaller businesses. What do you personally like about working with small businesses? Personalized attention, quick decision-making processes, high degrees of flexibility, perhaps? We know we appreciate those things from the small, women-run accounting firm that we use in Vienna, and chances are that your customers will appreciate the many advantages inherent to a small business as well.

4. Get organized

If organization is not your thing, then you might have cringed when reading the numerous references to the importance of being highly organized in this book. However, if you are not highly organized yourself, there are many tools and people who can help you. Being organized does not necessarily mean being tidy or orderly. Your pencils do not have to be sharpened and sit at a ninety degree angle to your notepad, unless that is important to you. When talking about being organized, we are referring to being able to find the important things in your business and to increase efficiencies by not wasting resources and having to spend time looking for the items you need.

In addition, we also recommend being organized in your finances and accounting so that you are aware of the specifics of your financial situation at all times and so that you can take advantage of all appropriate tax deductions available to you. Your desk might be messy, but if you can find what you need in a timely fashion, then that can work for you. If it takes you more than three minutes to find the physical document you are looking for, then you are probably in need of a better filing or organizing system. Perhaps you need to hire a young college student who can inexpensively organize your papers? Or how about installing some specific software that might make your life easier? Similarly, your computer files should be organized. Use the same three-minute rule. Can you find what you are looking for? On the computer you have the fantastic advantage of doing a search across files, but searching for a document, whether hard copy or electronic, is not the best use of your time. Remember that your time is your only resource, so use it wisely. Invest a few hours on a slow day to organize your folders, create new ones, do a clean-up, and find a system that works for you. Different solutions work for different people, but try to structure your files in such a way that is intuitive for you and that will make your search easier. If your system does not work initially, you can always change it later. Should you save all your price quotes in a "price quote" folder by month or should you save the price quotes in the specific client's folder? There is no right answer: find whatever works for you and stick to it.

In terms of finance and accounting, you should document and file all your receipts, expenses, as well as income in a timely manner. Some countries require you to do this monthly if you have to report your sales tax on a monthly basis. Be sure to comply with the rules and regulations in your country of residence. We think it is generally a good idea to record your expenses weekly or at least monthly, especially in case of the mileage you drive for business purposes. You may think you will remember where you drove on a specific day to visit a specific client and how far it was, but chances are you will not. The unfortunate consequence of that might be that you will have to go back through your calendar and/or notes to figure out your mileage. This will take you more time than simply logging your miles in your handy spreadsheet as soon as you sit down at the computer.

5. There is enough work for all of us

Some linguists tend to keep information about client acquisition ideas, strategies that work, and other important information to themselves because they are afraid to share it with colleagues. However, it is important for our professional and business development that we all share what we know with each other. The pie is big enough for all of us to do well, and we are stronger together than each on our own. If you are afraid that colleagues might steal your client just because you tell them your client's name, then you have not created a strong enough working relationship with your client. Significant growth is being projected for our profession in the coming years, so there is no need to be afraid that there will not be enough work.

6. You never know where your next client will come from

We cannot emphasize this enough. You should be prepared to meet and find clients in unusual places. While some customer acquisition ideas are better than others, the truth is that you really will not know if they work until you try them. Of course, this does not mean that you should show up at a random lawyer's office to pitch legal translation or interpretation services, but it does mean that you should keep your eyes and ears open for opportunities at all times. Stranger things have happened than language professionals meeting their next client at the gym, the coffee shop, or on an airplane. Whenever you are having a conversation with someone, your company, which is you, is also having a conversation. Ultimately, you are representing your business everywhere you go, whether you like it or not. Working for a large company gives you the distance between your personal and work life that you simply do not have as an entrepreneur. For instance: you work for a Fortune 500 company and you go to the Bahamas to have a fun weekend with friends and some pictures that show you drinking a bit too much are circulated on Facebook. This is not a big deal, because you are on vacation and having a good time, and as an adult, so you are certainly allowed to drink more than your share once in a while. Now, public perception will not be that your Fortune 500 company, let us call it the IceAgeNow company, is responsible for your behavior. No one will say "We will not hire IceAgeNow because Denise D'Amato was too drunk to drive in the Bahamas," and that is a good thing. An individual employee's behavior will not necessarily reflect poorly on the organization, unless the vice president of finance is embezzling funds from shareholders. As an employee, you can more easily separate work from your regular life. As a small business owner, you cannot. And since you are the one who will, most likely, be doing all the work, you need to take good care of your image. You can still have fun, but be aware that you are your company, and that your reputation is also your company's. You are all in one: CEO, shareholder, public relations coordinator, and face of the company.

7. Continuous learning

There is a reason that many certification programs such as the American Translators Association and statewide court interpreter certifications require professional development credits in order to keep their translation and interpretation certifications current. The same is true for many other high-level professionals, including attorneys. Even if you are not certified, you need to continue learning and developing your skills. This includes, first and foremost, conferences and workshops, but is not limited to those events. If you live in a relatively remote area or want to keep your professional development expenses low, take advantage of the internet by attending webinars, reading listservs, reading new literature in your area, and keeping abreast of any changes that affect you. Interact with other professionals and read language related publications. More than anything, you need to work on both your source and your target language by constantly expanding your vocabulary.

8. The software advantage

Does the word software make you cringe? We felt the same way for a long time. Our aversion dates back to high school in Mexico City, when our first-ever computer science class consisted of having to program an address book or such in Turbo Pascal (an old programming language). This was before the teacher had even explained how to turn on the monstrosity known as a personal computer back in 1991, and we were completely unfamiliar with the basics, including the mouse. As opposed to many other kids, who had tinkered with computers, hardware and software for years at home, our own household was decidedly devoid of emerging technologies, so we were quite unprepared for our computer science class. We taught ourselves everything we know about computing, and you can, too. Once you have learned a few basics, new software programs will make your life easier and more productive. And not to worry: you will not need any programming skills. All you will ever have to do is click the "install" button and go through the tutorial of your new program. If you do not like it or it does not suit your work style, move on to another program. However, give yourself the opportunity to grow and learn. Keep an open mind.

9. Surround yourself with good people

Judy's first mentor, who was the CEO of a large casino on the Las Vegas Strip, was a wise and entrepreneurial guy. He worked hard, played hard, and focused on one expensive hobby outside of work: horse racing. When Judy asked him for his top rule of the business world upon her graduation from business school, he said that his top rule is to surround himself with good people. It seemed like excellent advice ten years ago, and it sounds even better now. There is only so much work you can do yourself, and you have to have an inner circle of people you really trust. People in leadership positions within large corporations select their senior management teams with great care. When you run a small business, with or without employees, it could mean outsourcing services to professionals you really trust. It also means having an inner circle of friends, colleagues, and family who will give you honest opinions and with whom you can discuss anything business-related. These should not be people who will tell you what you want to hear, but people who will tell you the truth. While the truth might not always be pleasant, it is what you need to know in order to grow and thrive. There is nothing worse than giving someone your work to review and for them to come back with a glowing review and no changes at all. This either means that they are afraid to give you their opinion, afraid of hurting your feelings, want to tell you what you want to hear because they might have an ulterior motive such as getting work from you, or just do not care enough to give you a thorough analysis and critique of your work. Be careful to only approach people you know very well when looking for constructive criticism and review of your work.

10. No secrets

This year, Judy wrote an article about what translation and tennis have in common for the ATA *Chronicle*. At first glance, the topic seems like a stretch, but there are a lot of things to think about in terms of competitive sports and translation, or any business. We both played high-level junior tennis and were nationally ranked in the Top 5 as juniors. We played a few tournaments on the international tour before realizing we clearly did not have what it takes to make a good living as professional tennis players. Judy went on to play NCAA Division 1 college tennis on a full scholarship, while Dagmar decided to fully focus on academics.

A recent question posed by an interviewer reminded us of our life in tennis and about how many parallels there are between tennis and business. While there are strategies, tips, tricks, and best practices, there are no secrets. We are thrilled to share what we know, because we are firm believers that we should all share our collective knowledge. After all, we want all our colleagues to be successful and happy entrepreneurs. Sharing knowledge is a powerful thing that will make the profession stronger.

11. Editing twins

You do not have to have a biological twin to have an editing twin, but it certainly helps. In our case, we have always reviewed each other's work and developed a five-step quality assurance process. While we understand that twin translators might be far and few in between, it is quite necessary to find someone who can be your editing twin. You should find a trusted colleague in your same language combination and ideally in the same specialization. Set some ground rules, including the time commitment you are willing to make, and try to do an equal amount of work for each other. Our recommendation is not to charge each other, since that increases the complexity of your accounting. Put your agreement in writing so each party knows what the other party expects. You will find that there are many things that you can learn from your editing partner. By working together, you will not only deliver a better products for your clients, but you will also grow and learn.

12. The business of referrals

As entrepreneurs and small business owners, it is important that clients and friends give us referrals to other potential customers. While that is a critical factor in running a successful business, you should not forget that this equation works both ways and that you also need to refer other people. This does not have to be limited to the languages industry. While you should recommend fellow linguists for projects that you cannot accept for one reason or another, you should also think of other small businesses. For instance, your graphic designer might have done a fantastic job creating your logo. Why not recommend her? Or, if you have a friend who has a small law firm, why not keep some of his cards handy when someone asks if you know a good attorney? The more you give, the more you get, so do not forget about the flip side of referrals. You do not want to be known as the person who is constantly getting referrals but never giving any.

13. Become a speaker

One of the best ways to make a name for yourself within the languages community is to become a speaker at a professional event, workshop, or conference. With the exception of a lucky few, most of us do not truly enjoy speaking in public, especially in front of a large audience, but this is something you can work on and learn to love. If you have limited public speaking experience, your local association is a good place to start. Smaller, regional associations are traditionally in need of speakers, preferably those who are kind enough to donate their time. Approach the association's board of directors or the specific professional development committee and propose a topic that you feel strongly about, in which you are knowledgeable, and which would be of benefit to attendees. If there is interest on the organization's part, it is your professional obligation to present a top-notch workshop, regardless of whether you are being compensated or not. Spend a lot of time researching your subject and create a compelling presentation. You should time yourself carefully and rehearse the presentation at least three times. Be prepared to bring your own laptop and recruit friends and family to listen to your presentation at home before you give it in public. Ask for honest feedback and incorporate it into your workshop. While being a presenter is a tremendous amount of work, it establishes you as an expert and drastically increases your exposure. When you go to a conference or workshop, which individuals do you personally remember the most? Who stands out from the crowd at large conferences? It is usually the speakers.

14. Contribute articles to newsletters

Writing a contribution to a print or online newsletter is a good way to build your brand. There are several fantastic print newsletters that are distributed internationally, including the American Translators Association's *Chronicle* and the Institute of Translation and Interpreting's *Bulletin*. Most smaller and regional associations do not have the resources to print a physical newsletter, but almost all of them have quarterly newsletters in electronic form. Approach the editor of a newsletter that you read regularly and suggest a few topics that you could write about. Most editors at smaller newsletters have to work very hard to get articles for their publications, so they will most likely jump at the chance if your ideas fit their editorial guidelines and topics for that specific issue. Keep in mind that editors reserve the right to edit for length, style, grammar, punctuation, and clarity, and that your work may not appear in the newsletter exactly as you have written it. Consider asking the editor for a final proof before the newsletter is printed or published online so you can sign off on the changes that have been made. Online newsletters traditionally rank high in search results, so if a potential client does research based on your name, the contributions you have written to newsletters will come up in a prominent place in the search results. Hence, writing articles is a win-win situation for both you and the organization you are writing for. One caveat: show some humility in your writing and your interaction with the editor. While having your work critiqued is always difficult, you can learn from an established editor. You might think that your article is perfect, but it is quite likely that it is not.

15. Web 2.0 is your friend

The internet has brought professionals many advantages, including the ability to promote our services very inexpensively and effectively. Use the available technologies, including social media and professional networks, to your advantage. If you are not comfortable with some of the newer trends, including blogs, ask a friend or colleague for help or attend a seminar. The internet is the single best way to promote your services, and there is almost no learning curve. If you can write an e-mail, then you can handle most of the things we discuss in our social media and web 2.0 chapter.

16. Save money

While increasing sales year over year should be one of your main goals, you can maximize your profit, even if your sales stay stagnant, by decreasing your expenses. Most freelance translators have very little overhead thanks to home offices and no employees, but you can always save money. Analyze your expenses, group them into categories, and take a look at where you can save money. Learn to distinguish between needs and wants for your business. And do not be fooled by the term business expense. Just because you can write an expense off on your taxes does not mean the item or service is free.

17. Think outside the box

We are aware that you have heard this line before. It has been overused in the last decade of so, but the essence of this trite-sounding suggestion is still quite true. Being an entrepreneur means thinking outside the box, the lines, the house, or whatever your boundaries may be. That means that you might have to re-invent the way things are done or to create new, innovative ways of doing things. This is not always easy or pleasant, and you should be prepared for some opposition from either the establishment – organizations or fellow professionals – which is quite happy with the status quo. It is good and healthy to have some disagreement among peers, so do not be afraid to come forward with new ideas, even if they are not immediately popular. Our profession would not be what it is today without the collective wisdom of the people involved in it – professionals of all ages, walks of life, specializations, academic backgrounds, nationalities, and points of view. Always treat each others' ideas with professionalism and respect.

18. No excuses

As an entrepreneur, you are ultimately the only one responsible for when things go wrong with your business, and you can take all the credit when things go right. While this is a tremendous challenge, it also comes with enormous potential rewards. Have you ever worked on a project in a corporate environment only to not get the credit or the recognition you felt you deserved? If that has never happened to you, you are the exception. Now that you are on your own, you can get all the credit – and all the blame. There is no one to hide behind, no one to share blame with, unless you have a business partner or two, and you need to step up to the plate and assume responsibility. That is true even if a problem is beyond your control or was caused by a subcontractor. As the public face of the company and its owner, you are the company in the client's eyes. Make your customers appreciate that you are the decision maker if things go wrong. Acknowledge any mistakes, give a sincere apology, fix them quickly, and move on. If an error was made by one of your subcontractors, have a conversation about this issue with the subcontractor in a non-threatening way and decide where to go from there.

19. The importance of having goals

One of Judy's favorite professors in business school had a sign on his office door that read: "Goals without plans are just dreams." Judy walked by it every day, and we are not quite sure if the professor put up the sign in order to discourage lazy students from coming to see him with their self-created problems, or if he just meant it as an important guideline in life that students should remember. Either way, he was right. While the difference between a general idea in your head and a written document might seem small, it is actually quite significant. There is great power in making plans, both in the short term and in the long term, and sticking to them as much as possible. We are not suggesting you go out and spend dozens of hours creating elaborate mission and vision statements and spelling out every single goal for the next three years. We do, however, want to emphasize the importance of written goals. Be specific when you write down your goals, and set yourself a time limit for achieving these. The goals you set need to be achievable and realistic. For instance, setting the goal of increasing your sales by 200% in one year will set you up for failure. Take an hour or two to write down your plans and review them from time to time.

20. Give back

Giving back by doing volunteer work at your local or regional association is one of the most important things you can do for both your career and the profession. Associations would not exist if it were not for the hard work that is put in by volunteers around the world. Without professionals who are willing to work without pay, there would be no conferences, no professional development events, no mixers, and no linguist representation. While we can all agree that these associations are crucial to our success, not very many professionals donate their time by volunteering. We suggest increasing that percentage by donating your time, even if it is just a few hours a month. Please refer to our giving back chapter for more specific ideas.

We would like to thank you for purchasing this book and hope you have enjoyed reading it as much as we enjoyed writing it. We sincerely hope that this book's content will prove useful to you in your translation or interpretation work. We wish you much success on your Entrepreneurial Linguist journey.

ABOUT THE AUTHORS

Judy A. Jenner and Dagmar V. Jenner are identical twins and long-time professional linguists. They run their businesses, Twin Translations and Texterei, on both sides of the Atlantic. Judy is based in Las Vegas, NV, while Dagmar works out of Vienna, Austria. They work exclusively with direct clients, and their areas of specialization are business, travel and tourism, e-commerce, legal, and marketing. Their clients include businesses of all sizes, from Fortune 500 companies to small, family-owned companies on several continents.

They were born in Austria and grew up in Mexico City, where they attended the German School. Thanks to their international upbringing, they have enjoyed a multicultural and multinational life, and have turned their passion for languages into their profession.

Judy, the older twin, is a Spanish and German translator and community interpreter in Las Vegas, where she has resided since moving to the U.S. to attend college on a full tennis scholarship in 1995. She received both her undergraduate degree and her M.B.A. in marketing from the University of Nevada, Las Vegas (2001). She serves as the vice president of the Nevada Interpreters and Translators Association. Judy is a frequent speaker at conferences around the world, including the 50th Annual American Translators Association's Conference in New York City in 2009. Her workshops revolve around entrepreneurship, direct client acquisition, and web 2.0. She writes the monthly Entrepreneurial Linguist column for the American Translators Association's *Chronicle* and is also a frequent contributor to the Institute of Translation and Interpreting's *Bulletin* in the U.K. She serves on the advisory board of the specialized certificate in Spanish/English translation at the University of California, San Diego. She spends at least one month every year working with Dagmar in Vienna, Austria. Judy lives near

Red Rock Canyon in Las Vegas with her husband, Keith Anderson, and their dog, Luna.

Dagmar is a seasoned German, Spanish, and French translator and received the equivalent of a master's degree in French and Communications from the University of Salzburg, Austria, in 2000, and is currently enrolled in the master's program of conference interpreting (Spanish and French) at the Department of Translation Studies at the University of Vienna. Concurrently, she is writing her dissertation on feminist discourse in the work of Chilean author Isabel Allende. She is a respected expert on the German orthography reform (please visit her blog, www.neue-rechtschreibung.net) and web 2.0, and frequently presents workshops on those topics. Dagmar is the Assistant Secretary General of the nationwide UNIVERSITAS Austria Translators' and Interpreters' Association, where she spearheads the organization's public relations efforts. She is also the editor of the association's members' magazine, volunteers her time as a mentor to a newly minted entrepreneur, and shares her knowledge in consulting sessions. A passionate traveler, Dagmar always spends the summers with Judy in Las Vegas. Dagmar lives in Vienna, Austria, with her boyfriend, Thomas Gruber, and their cat, Junia.

Judy and Dagmar both enjoy sharing what they know with colleagues around the world. They pen a well-read translation blog, Translation Times, and offer consulting services to fellow entrepreneurs and small business owners. For more information, please visit: http://www.entrepreneuriallinguist.com/consulting-services/. To order additional copies of this book or to receive information about speaking engagements, please visit http://www.entrepreneuriallinguist.com/. The authors look forward to your comments, input, and suggestions. Contact: book@entrepreneuriallinguist.com.